PENGUIN BOOKS
BBC BOOKS

DOING BUSINESS IN JAPAN

Jonathan Rice first went to Japan as a schoolboy. After reading Japanese at Cambridge University, he returned to live and work there for almost ten years. During that time he managed the Japanese subsidiary of a major British electronics company and negotiated licences, joint ventures and import–export deals with Japanese partners. He even helped to bring two British musicals – *Jesus Christ, Superstar* and *Evita* – to the Tokyo stage. Since returning to Britain, Jonathan Rice has maintained his close links with Japan and travels to the country regularly. He is a consultant and lecturer on European business with Japan and runs his own cross-cultural business-briefing consultancy.

Jonathan Rice has written many books on popular music with Paul Gambaccini and Tim Rice, including the bestselling *Guinness Book of British Hit Singles*. He has also written three books on cricket and one on golf; *Play Bridge with Zia* in collaboration with Zia Mahmood; and two books based on TV sitcoms. He is m⋯⋯⋯⋯⋯⋯⋯⋯⋯ lives in Kent.

is married, has three children and

JONATHAN RICE

DOING BUSINESS IN JAPAN

PENGUIN BOOKS
BBC BOOKS

PENGUIN BOOKS
BBC BOOKS

Published by the Penguin Group and BBC Enterprises Ltd
Penguin Books Ltd, 27 Wrights Lane, London W8 5TZ, England
Penguin Books USA Inc., 375 Hudson Street, New York, New York 10014, USA
Penguin Books Australia Ltd, Ringwood, Victoria, Australia
Penguin Books Canada Ltd, 10 Alcorn Avenue, Toronto, Ontario, Canada M4V 3B2
Penguin Books (NZ) Ltd, 182–190 Wairau Road, Auckland 10, New Zealand

Penguin Books Ltd, Registered Offices: Harmondsworth, Middlesex, England

First published by BBC Books, a division of BBC Enterprises Ltd, 1992
Published with revisions in Penguin Books 1995
1 3 5 7 9 10 8 6 4 2

Printed in England by Clays Ltd, St Ives plc

CONTENTS

Introduction   1

1 An Introduction to Japan   3

2 Japan and Its People   19

3 The Work Ethic   39

4 The Structure of Japanese Industry   57

5 Exporting to Japan   73

6 Subsidiaries and Joint Ventures   93

7 Marketing, Sales Promotion and Public Relations   110

8 Negotiating with the Japanese   126

9 Survival Guide   143

  Further Reading   151

  Index   152

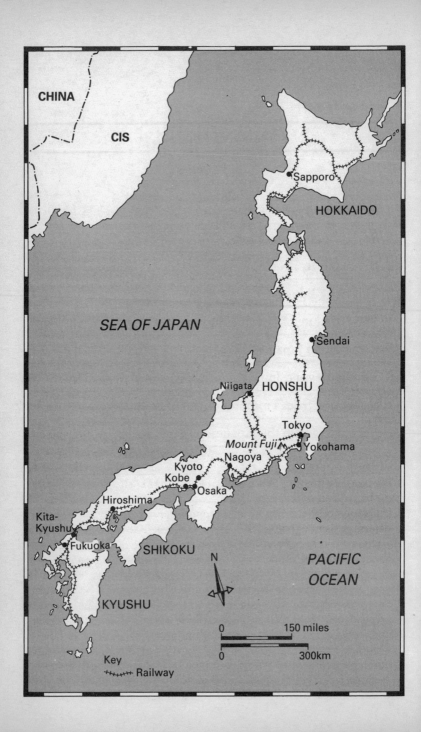

CHINA

CIS

SEA OF JAPAN

Mount Fuji

HOKKAIDO

Sapporo

Sendai

Niigata HONSHU

Tokyo

Yokohama

Nagoya

Kyoto
Kobe

Osaka

Hiroshima

Kita-
Kyushu

Fukuoka SHIKOKU

KYUSHU

PACIFIC
OCEAN

N

0   150 miles

0   300km

Key
+++ Railway

INTRODUCTION

In 1963, the American writer Boye de Mente published a book entitled *How Business Is Done In Japan* which was for many years one of the standard handbooks for business visitors to Japan. In those days, Japan was not an easy country with which to do business, and many international corporations decided not to make the effort required to break into this inscrutable, and probably not very profitable, market. The titles of de Mente's chapters show the attitude that prevailed 30 years ago: 'Problems of Joint Japanese-American Tie-Ups', 'Labour and Employee Problems', 'Problems of Distribution', 'Problems in Selling in Japan', 'Problems in Advertising', 'Problems in Public Relations', 'Problems in Printing', 'Psychological Problems of Americans in Japan'. The final paragraph of the final chapter is headed: Some Peculiarities. Clearly, problems and peculiarities are what you must expect if you want to do business in Japan.

Japan is, of course, a market with problems and some peculiarities, but then so are Germany, Italy and the United States of America. No company hoping to succeed in any of those markets would dive in without any preparation. All countries present problems to those who are not fully prepared, but, as the old marketing cliché tells us, every problem is an opportunity. Where once Japan was seen as a land of problems, today it can be a land of opportunity where any businessman determined enough to work out how to succeed can do so.

This book cannot give all the answers to all the questions that may be asked. What we hope it will do, is help take some of the mystery out of the way to reach the Japanese market, and give pointers towards what to do, and where to find out more, about Japan. The Japanese are not supermen. They are not beings of superior intelligence and greater determination than the rest of the world, although it would be equally futile to underestimate their business skills. Success in Japan, with Japan or against Japan means hard work, discipline and commitment because these are qualities the Japanese have in abundance. But they are qualities that are needed to succeed anywhere in the world. There is nothing really different about Japan.

When I first went to live and work there, in 1969, I was given one piece of advice which I have found very useful ever since, and which obviates the need for any other. It was simply, 'Don't be surprised.' I have, over the past two decades and more, been consistently unsurprised by all that I discovered about Japan, from the first Casio pocket calculator to the rules of banking, from Japlish advertising slogans to the price of a whisky in deepest Shinjuku. 'Don't be surprised' means, 'Don't have any preconceived ideas about Japan.' Follow this advice and everything becomes logical because all other concepts of logic are ignored. Before you start out on your campaign of doing business in Japan, forget everything you have already learned about exporting, licensing and overseas co-operation, and start from scratch all over again.

It's like pressing the Memory Clear button on your calculator before every new sum is done. If you do not clear the memory, you will get the wrong answer. Most people look at Japan from their own angle, so most people are surprised by what they see. The trick is to look at Japan from no angle at all. Press the Memory Clear button in your mind and just let the Japanese experience flow over you. You'll be surprised what a difference it makes.

Many people and organisations have given me a great deal of help in preparing this book, and it would be impossible to mention them all. However, in particular I would like to acknowledge the assistance of the Virgin Group, the Exports to Japan Unit of the Department of Industry, the Japan External Trade Organisation (JETRO) and the Commercial Department of the British Embassy in Tokyo; Dodwell Marketing Research Consultants for permission to reproduce statistics and tables from their book *Industrial Groupings in Japan* and the Toshiba International Foundation for allowing me to quote extracts from their 1991 conference on 'Technological Innovation and Society'; Kyoko and Graham Harris of Lloyds Bank in Tokyo for the most wonderful hospitality and Tony and Etsuko Grundy who made my research much more complete; finally, my agent, Mark Lucas, and my editor, Heather Holden-Brown, at BBC Books who smiled through all the problems I presented in putting this book together.

Jonathan Rice, December 1991

CHAPTER 1

AN INTRODUCTION TO JAPAN

Working with Japan, selling to Japan and doing business in Japan offers opportunities to British companies in all commercial sectors which cannot be ignored. Since the Second World War, Japan has become the world's second largest national market, after the United States. Japanese companies are active in practically all parts of the world and in practically all market sectors. Japanese consumers demand only the very best quality. The tariff and non-tariff barriers to international trade within Japan are virtually all gone and the market is as open to foreign goods and services as that of any other advanced nation. There is no reason any longer to believe that it is impossible to succeed there. Indeed, the business opportunities and disciplines that Japan offers combine to make success there in the 1990s the yardstick by which international success must be measured.

'It is a huge market, and a market moving in your favour,' says Tim Lloyd-Hughes of the Japanese financial house Nomura Securities, echoing the views of most other professional Japan-watchers. 'The consumer is becoming more overseas oriented, and foreign goods and services are being more eagerly accepted than ever before. Japanese companies are becoming easier to acquire. Everybody should be there.'

The old arguments are dead. The attitude of too many companies used to be: why bother? Japan is a very long way away, it is the hardest market in the world to break into, and the language is incomprehensible. Everything is unbelievably expensive and, what is more, the weather is far too hot and humid in the summer and there are no beaches worth sunning yourself on, so there is no incentive even to take a relaxed look at the country. The cities are ugly, noisy and overcrowded and the food odd. Surely any business executive would do better trying to break into the countries of what once was the Eastern bloc, or perhaps South Africa as their doors open once again. If a business works without reference to Japan, why change a winning system? If Japan does not need my business, why should my business need Japan?

This line of strategic thinking is no longer workable. Nobody disputes the wisdom of looking at new markets as they open their doors, but if you head for Vilnius or Johannesburg rather than Tokyo, the first competitors you will find there, already well established, will be the Japanese. The Japanese are not only a presence in Japan: they are competitors, customers, partners and suppliers to every country in the world. It is hard to think of a market sector in which they are not important players, nor of a geographical area where they have not already established themselves. In the words of Sir Peter Parker, Chairman of the Japan Festival of 1991 and a key figure in Anglo-Japanese trade and cultural relations for almost 50 years, 'The West cannot be the West without understanding the East.'

Japan was described as 'the reverse of Europe' by the first Jesuit priests to stumble ashore in the sixteenth century. To many Westerners 350 years later, it is still hard to understand, still inscrutable. Yet the Japanese see many similarities between the peoples of Britain and Japan, and think positively about the opportunities for business between our two countries, even though in historical terms the connection is recent, and in global terms the volume of trade is small.

The influence of Japanese activities on almost every area of business, in Britain and throughout the world, is self-evident. The motor industry, for example, has been revolutionised by Japanese concepts of quality and reliability in design, production and marketing, which create vehicles that customers love. The global success of the Japanese motor car has been sudden, unexpected and complete, so much so that Western manufacturers have taken Japanese production techniques, marketing and delivery methods into their hearts and their factories, even when it is clear that some of these aspects of Japanese motor manufacture are not relevant either to Japanese success or to Western companies trying to compete. Japan is a formidable competitor, yet there are also opportunities for co-operation in almost all sectors of industry, and for businesses which understand why Japan has succeeded.

The influence of Japan is felt in every business sector. Take hotels, travel and tourism: the most vigorous and cash-rich holiday-makers in the world are now the Japanese. The most successful companies cater for their particular tastes. Ask yourself why Japanese tour companies have much of their business. Why are particular hotels in London preferred by the Japanese? Why do they fly by some airlines more often than others? Take financial services – the City of London is the financial hub of Europe, and Japanese money plays an ever-increasing role in the City's transactions. The High Street banks may have got their acts together to a greater or lesser extent in both Britain and Japan, but even financial institutions that do not deal directly with Japanese customers need to know what is happening in Japan. The Tokyo market is a major influence worldwide and the magnet that attracts so much investment money from the West, and in turn invests so much money in Europe.

There are countless other examples we could find, taken from virtually any part of the business world. Even the teaching of English to foreigners is largely in Japanese hands these days. The lesson to learn is that you cannot expect to continue to succeed in your market place if you do not know what the Japanese are doing and how they are doing it.

Three Pillars of International Trade

The trilateral trade between Europe, Japan and the North American Free Trade Association (NAFTA) is the hub of international business. NAFTA, which is dominated by the United States, 'represents between one third and one half of the world market for most products', according to the British Overseas Trade Board. In 1993, 9.2 per cent of all British visible exports went there. However, 29.2 per cent of all Japan's exports went to the USA (over $100 billion), while only 15.6 per cent (around $56 billion) went to the EC, a larger market than the USA in both population and total buying power. Only $30 billion of the EC's total external exports went to Japan, leaving a trade deficit of around $26 billion in Japan's favour in 1993. This has resulted in what the Japanese government describes rather coyly as 'creating frustration among the EC countries. If the EC's trade deficit with Japan remains at past levels, this may create a strong move towards protectionism.' The Japanese view is that 'although the EC has well recognised that Japan has been making successful efforts to adjust its economic structure, it continues to express strong concern about the large trade imbalance persisting between Japan and the EC.' Some EC member countries would probably put it a little more strongly, even given the restraints of official diplomatic language.

Something like 60 per cent of world trade now involves at least one of the three pillars of world trade, and as long as these pillars are all roughly the same size and strength, the house of cards will

Table 1
Three Pillars: Visible Exports Between USA, Japan and EC
($ billions)

Exports to:	Japan	USA	EC	Total exports	Trade gap
Exports from:					
Japan		105	56	161	+76
USA	55		126	181	−40
EC	30	116		146	−36
Total imports	85	221	182	488	

The Japan/EC trade balance was $26 billion in Japan's favour. The Japan/USA trade balance was $50 billion in Japan's favour. Japan's exports exceeded her imports in this tripartite trade by 89 per cent.

Source: IMF/Bank of Tokyo, 1993 figures

not collapse. If one of the pillars is severely imbalanced, there is a danger of a breakdown in trade confidence, and a slowing down of the whole process of world trade. One of the pillars is, of course, severely imbalanced. Japan is running a massive trade surplus with both other corners of the triangle, a fact that not only shows up a probable reason for trade friction in the future but also highlights the huge potential there is for both European and American companies to counterbalance this inequality. Either Japan's economy must slow drastically to balance the trade with the EC and the United States, or else it must look to buy much more from both sources to even out the figures. As there is a danger that the first option could be enforced if the second is not entered into voluntarily, we can assume that Japan will in the future place an even stronger emphasis on encouraging imports and inward investment than it appears to be doing today. The Japanese market has never been more open for foreign business than it is now.

Germany is the most successful EC member state in terms of direct exports to Japan, and it also takes more imports from Japan than any other EC country. The UK runs second, with France a close third. By the first quarter of 1991, for the first time France was exporting more goods to Japan than Britain was, but the total of both countries' exports put together was less than Germany's exports to Japan and barely one fifth of the USA's exports to Japan. Britain's direct trade with Japan has been running at a large deficit for many years, but this deficit has not increased significantly in recent years. From 1986, when our imports from Japan were just over four times our exports to Japan, to the first half of 1994, when we imported £4.2 billions' worth of goods from Japan and sold £1.4 billion to Japan, the ratio has improved to around 3 to 1. There is still a great deal of room for further improvement.

The aim of the Department of Trade and Industry is to increase British exports to Japan from £2.65 billion in 1993 to £3.5 billion in 1996. A three-year campaign, Action Japan, will put the full power of the DTI behind the initiative, and there is no reason why these levels cannot be achieved, except that doing so relies on the enthusiasm and commitment of British exporters.

Japan is not just the single export target for the European exporter, any more than Britain is the only target in Europe for a Japanese exporter. Just as Britain forms a stepping-off point for other EC countries, so Japan can be viewed as just one country on the Pacific Rim. The Pacific Rim is an area of very wide diversity, comprising 14 countries with a population of about 500 million. The area is dominated by Japan, which accounts for seven-eighths of its GDP, but many of the other 13 nations are important markets in their own right: Brunei, Burma, Hong Kong, Indonesia, Kampuchea, Laos, Malaysia, the Philippines, Singapore, South Korea, Taiwan, Thailand and Vietnam. Japan is also the most important trading partner for most of the Pacific Rim countries, especially for the six (Brunei, Indonesia, Malaysia, the Philippines, Singapore, Thailand) that form the Association of South East Asian Nations (ASEAN).

There are no tariff or tax benefits in exporting from Japan to any other of the Pacific Rim countries, just as there are no particular advantages in setting up in one of the Pacific Rim countries to export to Japan, but in any plan of operations for East Asia, the whole area should be considered rather than individual target markets. European companies may benefit by adopting a regional policy, even if this does not involve the setting up of a headquarters in Japan, in the way that Procter & Gamble have done, for example, choosing Osaka as their centre of operations for the entire region. Hong Kong will be part of China from 1997, and all operations in East Asia will be affected by this change. Any strategy put into action now that does not take that simple but unavoidable fact into consideration is risking failure.

'Japan is not a traditional market for British industry,' says Paul Dimond, recently Commercial Counsellor at the British Embassy in Tokyo, citing Europe, the USA and the Commonwealth countries as the more normal historical destinations for British goods. However, these days he notes an increase in the number of corporate strategists visiting Japan from Britain. 'I welcome that very much.' Japan is getting easier to break into, he believes. 'On the whole, Japan is open. But the threshold for entry, particularly in industrial goods, is great, especially in management time. This is a highly competitive and dynamic market. The competition, domestic and foreign, is all here, and every newcomer needs all the help he can get.' This is not a market in which an unknown product is likely to break upon the market like a thunderclap. 'Japanese corporations are pretty good at scouting the world for what they want.

Table 2
United Kingdom Trade with Japan

EXPORTS				(£ millions)
Category	1988	1990	1992	1993
Chemicals	124	125	259	563
Textiles	112	106	99	67
Whisky	88	178	179	142
Machinery	102	140	478	648
Scientific instruments	95	106	89	97
Metals	130	162	24	96
Road vehicles	88	237	172	240

IMPORTS				(£ millions)
Category	1988	1990	1992	1993
Road vehicles	1420	1467	1498	1986
Telecoms, etc.	1078	948	873	887
Electric machinery	784	877	974	1207
Office machinery	877	940	1098	1221
General industrial machinery	791	749	378	365

Source: Overseas Trade Statistics of the United Kingdom

Catching the Japanese unawares with a good product they haven't heard of is rare.' But, with help, there is still a great deal of profit in the market. 'It is profitable at the end of the day,' says Dimond, 'and the length of that day has reduced. It used to be a seven-year market. Now it is a three- to five-year market.'

Japan is more than just an export target and more than just one export target on the Pacific Rim. The Japanese can also be suppliers, competitors and partners. Doing business in Japan does not mean only selling 'Made in England' products to this market. It is very likely to involve a degree of collaboration with a Japanese partner to achieve the goals set.

Table 2 shows that, among other things, Japan is already a very large market for Britain. In 1993, Britain's largest direct export market was the United States, with a total of £11,000 million worth of British goods crossing the Atlantic. The combined markets of Western Europe account for over half of our total exports, but among individual markets, Japan is firmly established as one of the biggest, accounting for 2.2 per cent of our export trade. There are already a large number of British companies doing very well in Japan.

Is It Too Late?

The obvious question for those who have not yet broken into the Japanese market is 'Am I too late?' As one partner in a leading London surveying practice has put it, 'Should we have started years ago?' The answer to that question is clearly 'Yes', because any head start would have been good news; but if the question implies that because you did not start five years ago, it is not worth trying now, then the implication is very wrong. It is never too late. 'If you want to get there, I shouldn't start from here, if I were you,' is not the right attitude. The DTI intends to do all it can to encourage British exports to grow vigorously, and the Japan External Trade Organisation (JETRO) is also committed to encouraging imports. All the external factors point to a greater opportunity to succeed in Japan, whatever your product or service, than ever before. All it depends on is your own company's commitment to doing business in Japan. You can get there from here.

The remarkable growth in the export of road vehicles from the UK to Japan over the past few years (see Table 2) is a perfect example of the 'better late than never' approach to Japan. In 1985 only £24 million worth of road vehicles were exported to Japan, compared with £864 million worth that came the other way. The Japanese sold 36 vehicles in Britain for every one we sold in Japan. By 1990 the sales of British cars had multiplied ten times, to £237 million, and although this is still a long way behind the £1,467 million we spend on Japanese-made cars, the trade deficit is now only six cars to one. What happened in those five years was that British car manufacturers took another look at a market that they had never attacked in quite the right way before. The Rover Group, then a subsidiary of British Aerospace, realised in the mid-1980s that the opportunities for imported vehicles in Japan were suddenly growing. Trade barriers were being lifted, and a major expansion of sales in Japan was now possible. Even though Rover cars had been available in Japan for well over twenty years (I remember going on a Land Rover sales trip to Kyushu in 1966), Japan was identified as a market which, after many years of allowing Rover to do no more than potter about on the fringes of profitability and success, could now be developed with a long-term strategy involving total commitment and support. By 1985 the Rover Group had taken over the import and distribution of their vehicles from local companies and had formed their own sales company, Rover Japan. Over the next few years Rover undertook many moves to improve the quality of its service and to increase the number of sales outlets in Japan. The Rover 800, the product of Rover's collaboration with the Japanese manufacturer Honda, was previewed in Japan before it was launched in Britain, a fact that was seen to underline Rover's commitment to the Japanese market. By 1993 this clear commitment had resulted in a growth of Rover's dealer network from 45 to 100, of whom two-thirds were now exclusive Rover Group dealers, where in the past none had been. Now the Rover 800 series, the Mini and the Discovery all sell well in Japan, and the total of almost 13,000 cars shipped to Japan in 1993 make it Rover's fourth biggest export market by sales volume. As the company says, 'In Japan the long-term view is paramount. The market environment is not receptive to sharp growth; this is seen to be counter to proper standards of customer service.' The Rover Group may have come late to the market, in terms of really understanding what is needed to succeed in Japan, but it has still managed to carve out a strong market position for itself. It is never too late to do business in Japan.

The Qualities Needed to Succeed in Japan

What are the qualities that are needed to succeed in Japan? Will a person who has done deals in other parts of the world automatically be successful there? Does a company need to have a range of 'Japan specialists' before it can hope to break the barriers of inscrutability which will confront it?

When people with experience of Japan are asked what is the prime quality needed in a person who must deal with the Japanese, the response is always the same – patience. By far the most important personal characteristic for anybody in Japan is the ability to be patient, to be able to control the emotions and not to expect a sale, or even a reply to a question, overnight. Coupled with patience, however, is persistence. A passively patient person, waiting by a telephone or a fax machine for a reply from a Japanese company, will probably be waiting in vain, and will certainly not succeed in the long term. A persistent person, who is not rude but never gives up, will win the respect of the Japanese, who are always looking to build relationships with people and with organisations before they are willing to do business with them. It is worth remembering that there are those who would say that patience and persistence are not only *the* most important qualities needed for success in Japan, they are also the second, third, fourth and fifth most important qualities. Companies as well as their representatives must have both in plentiful supply. 'You have got to be patient, you really have,' says Tim Bridgman, President of John Swire & Sons (Japan) and also President in 1991 of the British Chamber of Commerce in Japan. 'It is no good being a hands-on, let's-make-this-happen-tomorrow type. You need patience and the ability to listen.'

Dr George Newns, head of British Telecom Japan, identifies the two options for choosing a person to do business in Japan. 'You can hire a linguist and hope to train him in the business. Or you choose a man who knows the company, and who you hope and expect will be able to cope with Japan.' In his opinion, 'the latter opinion is always better.'

The Japanese will respect a person who knows his produce, his company and his market. They will not be interested in anyone who is not fully briefed, even if he can conduct all his business in Japanese.

'Japanese people like *gaijin* (foreigners) who follow a career pattern like their own, in other words, have a long career history with one company,' says Newns. 'If you do not know your business, and, more importantly, if you have not built up the relationships within your own company to make you more effective, your credibility is gone. You cannot refer back to headquarters every time.' Most foreigners resident in Japan will agree. One Tokyo-based British businessman even went so far as to say that if he had been selecting a candidate for his position, 'I wouldn't have chosen me. I do not speak Japanese and I came from outside the company to take up this position. From my track record, I should not have been a candidate. However, I am glad they overlooked details like that.'

Japanese linguists are in short supply in Britain, and the universities are not producing very many more. Many graduates in Japanese either go straight back into the academic life or else head for the City to make their fortunes at the earliest possible age, so the pool of Japanese linguists available to go into industry is very small indeed. However, they are around. Mike Barrett, who heads up the Japan office of the international executive search company GKR, believes there is a pool of *gaijin* talent in Japan which has grown enormously in the past few years. 'There is also a lamentable wastage of this talent. People want to stay here, but their companies rotate them. I have people coming out of my ears who want to stay on, but it is difficult to get them the top jobs. Foreign companies could use this pool of talent much more than they do.'

There are a number of personal characteristics which will make a person more likely to succeed in Japan, although it should not be assumed that anybody not fitting the ideal profile will be a failure. Apart from patience, persistence and a strong background within the company he represents, it has to be admitted that the next important qualification for a Japan representative is that he is male. We will talk in greater detail about women at work in Chapter Three, but in the meantime it is worth noting that Japan is still essentially a man's country and, all other factors being equal, a foreign male will fare better than a foreign woman, especially on an initial trip to the country. There are, of course, many examples of women being hugely successful, but they are still the exception rather than the rule.

The requirements for a visiting foreign salesman, who deals with Japan as part of his patch, differ from the requirements for a Japan-based executive. When thinking about placing someone permanently, there are a number of quite separate personal considerations about family, a wife's job and children's education, which are not important in looking for a UK-based representative. However, it is no good sending someone too young to have these commitments and imagining he will perform well in Japan. Below the age of 30 to 35, a foreigner would probably not be considered sufficiently experienced or sufficiently senior to operate effectively. It is important, though, not to appoint somebody with too grand a title on his business card. Like is expected to deal with like, and a managing director will have to speak to a managing director, at least to begin with. This would be too high a level in a Japanese company to conduct everyday business, so, unless the British company is quite small, it is far better to work at the manager level than at the director level.

A person who is too decisive is not particularly welcome in Japan. The Japanese decision-making process is a group process (see Chapter Three) and the Japanese are not generally happy with somebody who makes an instant decision without even pretending to refer the matter to his colleagues. Doing this can be seen as arrogant and unhelpful. That is not to say that any visitor to Japan must refer everything back to headquarters before agreeing with a Japanese proposal. It is taken for granted that he has a range of authority within which he has no need to talk to his colleagues. However, if a new idea is tabled, or a condition suggested which is clearly outside the original range of the discussions, a decisive and immediate 'yes' or 'no' is not appreciated, even if the foreign visitor knows he can take the decision with impunity. Some pretence at referral to colleagues is seen by the Japanese as the right way to maintain good relationships within any company. They believe, with reason, that such a discussion, even by telephone or by fax, will help prevent anybody back in Britain feeling antipathy towards a deal brought back from Japan. Antipathy towards a deal usually develops into antipathy towards the company at the other end of the deal, and that would provide a rock on which the business relationship could founder. The Japanese will try to avoid such a situation arising if at all possible.

There are other qualities which help in Japan. A willingness to try anything, whether it is raw squid, a new delivery schedule or *karaoke*, is certainly important. The need to be proud of your company but self-deprecating about your own part in it is also necessary. The ability to be aware of what is happening, and not to criticise even if you do not understand, is another quality. It is a part of being patient and persistent. 'You need a sense of the lunatic,' says Tim Bridgman. George Newns would add that you need, 'a hell of a good sense of humour.' You certainly do. This is a useful defence mechanism against not understanding what is happening. Laughing at mystery makes it less threatening. The wry smile is a common expression on the faces of *gaijin* in Japan.

Above all, Paul Dimond at the Embassy believes that, 'You must send your best people to Japan. The Japanese send their best people to Britain.' He cites as an example of this the fact that Mitsui & Co.'s 1991 annual report shows that the head of Mitsui Europe, based in London, is a Vice-president of Mitsui and outranks the head of Mitsui in the United States.

Ben Thorne, formerly Commercial Counsellor at the British Embassy and now a consultant on Japan trade, has some straight-forward advice. 'Be yourself. If you are reliable, honest and if you know your stuff, you will be all right. They are quick to spot any falsity.'

Nemawashi

The Japanese have a word, *nemawashi*, which literally means 'binding the roots'. This is a horticultural term, transplanted into common business usage, that describes the process of preparation for replanting a tree or other plant successfully. Before anything can be done, there must be the thorough preparation of digging around and binding up the roots of the tree. In business Japanese today, *nemawashi* has come to mean the informal process of canvassing opinion and looking at the problem from all angles before reaching a decision.

The Japanese are entirely convinced of the virtues of preparation. The old English 'amateur' ideal (which probably never really existed, but the English like to pretend it did) of the man whose natural talents allow him to succeed without practice or preparation is alien to Japan. Ben Thorne puts it bluntly: 'However well you prepare, your Japanese opposite numbers will have prepared better.'

There is no point in coming to Japan in the hope that you will make a useful contact, or in an attempt to off-load some likely looking items that have been cluttering up the warehouse for months. Coming to Japan unprepared is a complete waste of money. You must bind the roots first.

Nemawashi involves understanding the market, and understanding the place your product could take in the market. It also involves setting up meetings before you reach Japan. These can usually only be arranged with an acceptable introduction. Cold calling just does not work. However, the Japanese are happy to build on any small relationship, and will certainly be happy to help a newcomer, so even a casual acquaintance may be enough to set the ball rolling. Any first visit to Japan must be with a firm objective. Try to find out as much as you can in advance, and then act on that information to create a worthwhile and constructive visit. It is going to be expensive, however well you plan it, so any time lost through poor preparation will be money out of your pocket.

This all seems so obvious that it is hardly worth repeating. However, many a first-time visitor to Japan has come so unprepared as to make one wonder how he even made it on to the aeroplane at Heathrow. There seems, in some cases, to be a feeling that the country is so different and so far away that the normal rules cannot possibly apply. Fortunately, they do. The normal rules of preparation, market research and careful planning of the time available, which are followed when dealing with Germany, France or any more familiar market, still work in Japan. The answers may be different, but the same questions need to be asked.

The Japanese Market

Japan, with a population of over 124 million, is now the second largest economy in the world. The economy has grown at a rate of over 4 per cent per year since the late seventies, and grew at an even faster rate before that. Its GNP is around $2.5 trillion, with a GNP per head of over $21 000, compared with just under $20 000 per capita for the United States and just over $13 000 for Britain. Japan has over 52 million motor vehicles on its roads, compared with 23 million in Britain. It produced 13 million vehicles in 1989, two million more than the United States, and almost 10 times the production of Britain (1.6 million in 1989). Unemployment and inflation rates have consistently run below those of even the best of the Western nations, and its balance of payments continues to show a massive surplus. Wholesale prices stand well below the 1985 levels. The country is virtually self-sufficient in food, despite a massive drop since the Second World War in the number of people involved in agriculture, and in 1989 it began work on 1.7 million dwellings, almost eight times as many as in Britain. The economy is thriving, despite recession and financial and political scandals, and Japan will continue to be an essential market for British products and services across all sectors of the economy.

By the end of 1989, direct investment by foreign countries in Japan totalled $15 654 million, of which $599 million (3.8 per cent) came from Britain. There were by then 336 British or partly British companies operating there. This compares with $7910 million (50.5 per cent) invested by American corporations across 1494 Japanese companies. Britain's investment is comparatively large, behind only Switzerland, The Netherlands and Germany apart from the USA, and all three of those countries have fewer subsidiary companies in Japan. The average investment per company into British subsidiaries was $1.8 million (almost exactly £1 million), compared with $5.3 million in each American subsidiary, $5 million in each Swiss one, $4.3 million in the case of The Netherlands and $2.5 million for Germany. The image which emerges from these Japanese Ministry of Finance figures is of a large number of small British companies, in contrast to a smaller number of larger subsidiaries of other foreign companies. Britain comes across once again as a nation of shopkeepers.

The Japanese consumer is one of the richest and most powerful in the world. Apart from being the best dressed and the best fed, he or she is also used to getting the best. 'You must never mention quality as a virtue. It is taken for granted,' said one hopeful exporter of fashion accessories who was sitting, rather disconsolately, in the airport departure hall at Narita after a 10-day introductory visit to Japan. 'I cannot believe the importance they place on politeness and service. And the packaging! It seems to be second nature to them that their customer is God.' *Kyakusama wa osama* (the customer is king) is a very commonly heard saying in the retail business.

It would be wrong to assume, however, that only by following the Japanese rules can a company hope to be successful. When Coca-Cola was first introduced into Japan, the common perception was that the Japanese could never be trained to like this strange-tasting foreign drink. The Coca-Cola Company even went so far as to decide not to use the infamous Japanese distribution networks to get their unwanted foreign product to the market, and set up their own system. The result was that within a short while Coca-Cola became the largest selling soft drink in Japan. The only truly Japanese thing the company did was to show a real commitment to the market, and never keep their eye off the winning-post. The same could be said of McDonald's, whose product was considered by the experts to be hopelessly unsuited to the Japanese diet. Within months, their Ginza store had become the single biggest McDonald's outlet in the world, and the company has never looked back.

Japan is Changing

Japan is different. 'Think of Japan as a different culture. Don't go with any preconceived ideas,' says Chris Moss, Marketing Director of Virgin Atlantic Airlines. But is Japan changing? Are its differences becoming less different?

'There are the same carp swimming in the palace moat,' according to Dick Large of British Aerospace, who returned to Japan in 1991 after several years away, 'and the same faces in the lobby of the Capitol Tokyu Hotel, but underneath I suspect it is all deeply different.' Wherever you turn in Japan, you will hear the words 'Japan is changing.' If they come from a Japanese, they are spoken with a mixture of pride and determination. Japan is changing from the immediate post-war economic boom, achieved at the cost of international trade friction and environmental devastation, and is now moving into a period of expansion of the welfare of its people and the internationalisation of its economy. If the words are spoken by a foreigner, the implication is often 'Japan is changing and it's a good thing too. It's about time they had their come-uppance.'

'This is pure wishful thinking,' says Graham Harris, General Manager of Lloyds Bank in Tokyo, and a man with twenty-five years' experience of the country. 'Every time the Japanese have faced a problem, they have come out of it stronger than before. The oil shock of the early 1970s led to fuel-emission control technology. President Nixon's visit to China, which was a traumatic event for Japan at the time, merely opened a huge market for Japan. The ever-strengthening yen has forced manufacturing industry to trim costs by streamlining production processes. This has made Japanese industry even more competitive.' He believes that the idea that some crisis will arise to force Japan's juggernaut off the road is wrong. 'They thrive on adversity. All Japanese exporters quickly worked out how they could still make profits at ¥120 = $1 and four years ago had strategy planning for ¥100 = $1. The idea that a couple of yen makes any difference is ridiculous.'

Ben Thorne agrees. 'Japanese management tries to prevent problems from happening, while Western managers look for problems to solve. Ask a Western manager what he enjoys, and he may well say, "Crisis management." A Japanese manager will ask, "What sort of man is this who allows a crisis to happen?".' The Japanese foresee change and work with it to create smooth progress.

'Yes, Japan is changing and will continue to change rapidly,' says Harris. 'But people assume that this means that Japan cannot go on being successful for ever. That is where I part company with them. Why should Japan stop being successful? Yes, the Japanese are changing on the surface, but not underneath.' He adds one more word of caution: 'The Japanese have been very successful despite their limited knowledge of foreign countries. Imagine how much better they will do as they travel more widely.'

'You cannot ignore Japan, because Japan will not ignore you,' he believes. 'But it is no good being here just to plant a flag, because all that will do is reconfirm your prejudices against Japan, that Japan is too difficult a market. If you are going to come here, come. But if you are half-hearted about it, stay away.'

CHAPTER 2

JAPAN AND ITS PEOPLE

Geography

Japan is an archipelago in the North Pacific, consisting of four main islands and hundreds of smaller ones, about 130 kilometres (90 miles) at its nearest point from the Asian mainland. It stretches from approximately 45°N to 30°N and from 130°E to 145°E. The north-south position is very similar to that of the United States, which stretches from the 49th parallel to roughly 30°N, if we ignore Florida. New Orleans is at 30°N. The whole country is further south than most Europeans would imagine: 45°N is the same latitude as Bordeaux; 30°N puts the southern tip of Kyushu on the same latitude as Cairo.

The four main islands are Hokkaido, in the north; Honshu, on which Tokyo, Osaka and several of the largest cities in Japan are situated; Shikoku, the smallest and least populated of the main islands; and Kyushu in the south. The Ryukyu Islands, which include Okinawa, stretch out some way to the south of Kyushu. They were returned to Japan in 1972 from post-war American control, and are so completely different from mainland Japan in their climate, economic development and even the history of their peoples, that it is worth remembering that not all of what is written in this book will apply directly to Okinawa.

The climate of Japan ranges from sub-Arctic in the north to subtropical in the south. The island of Hokkaido and the Japan Sea coastal area of Honshu suffer from very cold winters with heavy snowfalls, yet most of the country is part of Asia's monsoon belt, with high rainfall and high humidity in the summer to encourage the growth of rice as a staple crop. In Japan, the four seasons are marked by sharp contrasts in the climate, but also by a regularity and predictability of climate which is a new experience for English people used to the possibility of snow in Derbyshire in June. Temperatures in Tokyo range from an average of 3°C (37°F) in February to 27°C (81°F) in August, but even in January and February the temperature rarely falls much below freezing. In the summer months, the biggest problem is humidity rather than heat. The Japanese summer, like a

Japanese breakfast, is something most foreigners try to avoid. It begins in mid-June, with a rainy season of about four weeks. From mid-July until mid-September, the sticky heat of the Japanese summer is all-pervading: it is worse, incidentally, in Osaka, where the temperatures rise a couple of degrees higher and the humidity is no less. Air-conditioning is essential to survive the Japanese summer; fortunately, practically every public building, private home and motor car is fully equipped these days.

In Tokyo, the winter is comparatively mild, but very dry. The biggest problem in January and February is the cold, dry air which creates skin problems and a massive build-up of static electricity. During these winter months, door knobs, lift buttons, handshakes and even kisses are likely to create small shocks. It snows occasionally in Tokyo, although snow is rare on the plains in the Osaka area or further south. When it does snow, usually quite late on in the winter, around the beginning of March, it can snarl up the public transport system as surely as it does in England. It is heartening to know that the 'wrong sort of snow' falls in Japan too: in the bad old days of non-tariff barriers in the 1970s, the reason given for a Japanese refusal to go along with international standards governing the design and manufacture of skis was that a different kind of snow falls in Japan. But it resembles British snow in that it can throw the capital's transport systems into complete confusion.

One aspect of the country which takes even more getting used to is that it lies on an earthquake belt. Earth tremors happen all the time, but most of them are not felt by the population. Earthquakes are very rare in western Japan. However, anybody who stays in and around Tokyo for more than a month or so, or any regular visitor to the country, is very likely to feel one. The last devastating earthquake in the Tokyo area was in September 1923, when the cities of Tokyo and Yokohama were all but destroyed by the massive shock and the fires it caused; 140 000 people died. Japanese seismologists have a gloomy theory that major earthquakes can be expected to recur about every 60 years, so Tokyo is overdue for another big one. However, there is every expectation that another earthquake on the scale of the 1923 one would have nowhere near the effect that it had then. Buildings have become increasingly 'earthquake proof', beginning with the theories of Frank Lloyd Wright, whose Imperial Hotel was one of the few buildings in central Tokyo to survive the 1923 quake. There is clear evidence that there would be neither the collapse of buildings nor the outbreak of fires if another earthquake happened today. Those who have experienced a tremor when in the restaurant at the top of the Hotel New Otani tower are able to vouch for the fact that, although there was a great deal of swaying and a few glasses of spilt wine, the building remained entirely safe and there was no danger at any time. Earthquakes are a fact of life in Japan. They should not affect your business there.

Japan, with a total land area of 378 000 square kilometres (145 900 square miles) is about 1.6 times the size of the United Kingdom, but just one twenty-fifth the size of the United States. Seventy-two per cent of its land, an area larger than Britain, is officially designated mountainous, so pretty well the entire population lives and works on the remaining 28 per cent, about 100 000 square kilometres (37 000 square miles). In Britain about 20 per cent of the land is uninhabitable, leaving about 200 000 square kilometres (74 000) square miles for our use. Japan's population is 124 million, just over double Britain's, so it does not take a great mathematician to work out that if twice the population is crammed into an area half the size, there will be four times the population density. This is the most immediately obvious point about Japan's geography, and the one that most affects the way business is done there.

History

Japan has been a single political entity for longer than any other country in the world. The Japanese celebrated the 2600th anniversary of the first emperor's accession in 1940. The date that the Emperor Jimmu came to the throne is traditionally given as 660 BC, but the true date for the first emperor's accession is several hundred years later than that, probably in the first or second century AD. The first mention of Japan in Chinese histories occurs in AD 57, and no single ruler seems to have been acknowledged in Japan until the fourth century AD. Whatever the true date, the present Emperor Akihito can trace his direct line back for more than 1500 years. The imperial family has wielded no real political authority for most of that time, but has always been revered by the people and used by the rulers of the day as a symbol of their legitimacy. For many years in early feudal times, there was a regular practice of marrying the emperor to the daughter of the chief minister, and then, when a son was born, insisting that the emperor abdicate in favour of his infant son, the grandson of the chief minister.

The Japanese have always considered themselves a race apart because, from the earliest days until 1945, there was no successful invasion of their country. Buddhism came to Japan in the seventh century AD, but it was a peaceful, cultural invasion which did not involve the immigration of new peoples. The Mongols tried to invade in 1274 and again in 1281, but were defeated largely by the weather, regarded by the Japanese as 'divine winds' (*kamikaze*). The Japanese themselves, unlike most European nations, did not feel the need to conquer other countries, at least until they allowed themselves to be influenced by the West in the late nineteenth and twentieth centuries. (The great feudal leader Toyotomi Hideyoshi began an invasion of Korea in 1592, but it was not successful.) For 250 years, until 1868, Japan even went so far as to close its doors completely (*sakoku:* closed country), executing all foreigners who came there, and all Japanese foolish enough to return after leaving the country. Even fishermen swept out to sea and shipwrecked in the Philippines or Korea would be killed if they dared to return to Japan.

It was the West, initially in the person of Commodore Matthew Perry of the US Navy, who forced an end to the exclusion policy and in so doing brought about the collapse of the feudal system which had existed under the Tokugawa shoguns, rulers of Japan since the fall of Osaka Castle in 1615. In only 125 years since then, Japan has turned itself from being a very backward feudal nation into the most thriving economy in the world, perhaps the most avid international trader of all. Yet its political power and influence remain minimal.

Politics

Japan is a multi-party democracy, with universal suffrage for people aged 20 and above. The emperor is head of state, but performs merely a ceremonial role. The government is in the hands of a prime minister and his cabinet, which is made up of members of the largest party in the parliament, or Diet. The Japanese Diet is bi-cameral, with a House of Representatives consisting of 512 members, and a House of Councillors, the upper house, consisting of 252 members. The House of Councillors is an elective assembly, with half the members standing for election every three years on a basis of both constituency and national votes. The House of Representatives can, like the British House of Commons, be dissolved by a government wishing to hold an election. The electoral constituencies each elect between three and five members, not necessarily all from the same party.

It used to be said of the Holy Roman Empire that it was not holy, Roman or an empire. Similarly, the Liberal Democratic Party of Japan is neither liberal, democratic nor a party. Its politics are not liberal but conservative, and determinedly interventionist when it wishes to be. It is not democratic, in that it hardly listens to the voice of the people. Prime Minister Toshiki Kaifu was forced to resign as leader of his party at the end of 1991, despite landatory opinion polls, largely because he was trying to bring in much needed reforms to the political system that would have had the effect of weakening the LDP's stranglehold on Japanese politics. Last, it is not a party because it began as an amalgamation of two parties and is now a loose federation of five major factions who each try to put their views above those of their rivals. It had long been said that the LDP did not need an opposition as it opposed itself more effectively than the official opposition parties ever did, but the election of 1993 suddenly pushed the LDP into opposition itself and put an end to over forty years of one-party rule.

After the 1993 election the LDP held 206 seats in the House of Representatives. Although it could not hold on to office, it was still by some distance the largest party in the chamber, with more seats than its three main rivals combined. However, more than three main rivals did combine against the LDP to force the party's hand and challenge its forty-year monopoly of power. The Komeito, or 'Clean Government Party', held 52 seats, the Japan Renewal Party (JRP) held 62 seats, the Japan New Party held 37 seats, the Social Democratic Party held 74 seats, the Democratic Socialist Party (not to be confused with the Social Democratic Party) held 19 seats, the Liberal Party seven and the 'Former Reform Group' (Kyu-Kaikaku no Kai) four. The LDP was forced into opposition, and a coalition has held uneasy sway over the country since 1993. In its first eighteen months of office, there had already been three different prime ministers.

There are two things to know about Japanese politics. The first is that foreigners with strong views on Japanese politics are not appreciated. The second is that the years of LDP rule have been extremely beneficial to industry in general, and the new governments have made no attempt to make any significant changes to the relationship between government and industry. It works.

Society, Group Dependency and the Power of Relationships

Because Japan is such a crowded island, the Japanese have never been used to being alone or working alone. The Western concept of individuality is a strange one to them. Japanese society, and therefore Japanese business, is built on relationships with other people. In Japan, it is impossible to live in isolation. There is always somebody else nearby who has to be considered. In that way it is almost the opposite of the American ideal of a man alone, taming the wide open spaces. There are no wide open spaces in Japan. A man has not gotta do what a man's gotta do, he's gotta do what the group's gotta do, and this is an entirely natural way of life.

John Donne could have been thinking of the Japanese when he wrote, 'No man is an island, entire of itself,' except that in the early seventeenth century he had probably never heard of Japan. The Japanese are not 'entire of themselves,' and the overwhelming group mentality that pervades every action and every plan needs to be remembered all the time.

The Japanese see themselves in terms of other people, rather than as individuals in their own right. Ask a Japanese who that person over there is, and he may reply, 'I am his friend.' A Westerner would probably say, 'He is my friend,' putting himself at the centre of the relationship. A Japanese tends to describe himself in terms of the rest of society. It is as though he would have no existence if it were not for other people. A Japanese business colleague put it very clearly when he said that the Japanese are analogue, but Westerners are digital. At first, I thought he had got it the wrong way round: surely the electronically advanced Japanese are the digital ones while the backward Europeans are analogue. But no; he repeated the assertion that the Japanese are the analogue race. An analogue clock tells the time by means of the relationship between the big hand and the little hand. If there is only one hand on the clock face, you have no real idea what the time is. The relationship also explains what the time was a minute ago, and what it will be in one minute's time, because the clock face is a third part of the relationship which tells us the time. The hands cannot go from 8 to 10 without passing through nine. A digital clock, in contrast, tells you clearly what the time is now, but that is all. It has no hands and no face. It is accurate but without reference to anything else. A Japanese thinks of himself as part of the whole: a Westerner does not.

A Japanese businessman will introduce himself by saying, for example, '*Watanabe Shoji no Gyomubu no Tanaka desu.*' This would translate into English as, 'I am Mr Tanaka of the Sales Administration Department of Watanabe Trading Company.' In Japanese, Mr Tanaka has told us first the name of his company (the most important definition of his job, and the most important relationship of his working life) and then his department within the company before he has told us his name. He has not mentioned his rank within the company at all, although that will be evident from the business card (*meishi*) he hands over as he makes his verbal introduction. In English it is the other way round. A British businessman would introduce himself by saying, 'My name is Smith. I am Manager of the Export Department of Bloggs International.' If you ask an Englishman what he does for a living, the chances are he will say, 'I am an accountant' or 'I am a lawyer' or 'I am a sheet-metal worker'. If you ask a Japanese, he will say 'I work for Honda' or 'I work for Mitsubishi' and you may not find out for some time what his personal skills are. The group is important, as is the reassurance that he is part of the group. His job really is to work for Honda or Mitsubishi. It is not being an accountant or a salesman. His real skills are in the way he has built up his network of relationships for the benefit of his company.

The Japanese start building relationships from the moment they are born. They are immediately somebody's son or daughter, somebody's grandchild, perhaps somebody's younger brother or sister. The child is immediately introduced into a vertical society, where rank is everything; and much rank is decided by the accident of date of birth. There are different words in Japanese for older and younger brother and older and younger sister. Relationships build through schooldays and university days and are carried into the working environment. It is not just 'the old school tie' as understood in Britain: the relationships continue to be very important, and somebody who was at the same university as you but a year or two ahead will be deferred to throughout life. A foreigner is a *gaijin*, literally 'outsider', somebody who does not belong to a group.

As an aside, it is worth noting that some of the most popular leisure-time activities in Japan are those in which a person must look in on himself or herself and achieve something alone, without relying on the group. It is as though, just occasionally, the Japanese want to put the pressures of relationships on one side. Sports like fishing and judo are hugely popular, as is the Western sport which most obviously defines the conflict of man against himself: golf. Other leisure activities like *ikebana* (flower arranging) or photography are essentially one-person pastimes too; but, of course, the Japanese join clubs to form relationships with other people who enjoy their time off in the same way as they do.

A Japanese is defined by his relationship to other people. We commonly use relationship terms like 'father' and 'grandma' and 'boss', but, where we would use given names, it is the norm in Japan to address other people by their relationship with the speaker. The Japanese call each other 'elder brother', 'section chief' or 'classmate' rather than Hiroshi or Kazuko or Suzuki-san. As a general rule, the formal non-family relationship takes precedence over the family one. A son who works in the family firm will refer to his father as 'Mr President' rather than as 'father'. A Westerner is, of course, outside this formal structure. He has not been a classmate or elder brother, and his only relationships within Japan will be in his working life, as employee, colleague or, perhaps, Mr President. However, he should never forget the importance the Japanese attach to relative positions in the hierarchy, even if they are of little importance to him.

It will be difficult to build new relationships with the Japanese, not only because they need time to assess your commitment to them and to their business, but also because on many occasions a new business relationship can only be formed by breaking an old one. 'The Japanese hate breaking relationships,' says Andrew Lawson of the CBI. 'It is as traumatic as a divorce.' There have been many cases, he believes, of a British company having the right product at the right price and the right time, but being unable to sell into Japan because their potential customers could not break the longstanding relationship with their present suppliers.

A Westerner does not have the ready-made relationships which enable the Japanese to place him in their hierarchy, and allow them to decide how to deal with him. He has not been to a Japanese school or university, he does not work in a Japanese company and he has not the status or obligations that all Japanese take with them through life. Furthermore, the Japanese have not built up with him the atmosphere of complete trust that is needed to make a relationship flourish. That does not mean that they think that all Westerners are trying to cheat them, or will steal their pencils as soon as their backs are turned. It merely means that the natural understanding, the assumptions based on a shared heritage and the simple interpretation of words and signals is not there, so trust is hard to build.

The Western businessman will be faced with a group, and his first responsibility is to build a relationship between his group (his company of which he is the representative) and the Japanese group. It is neither sensible nor correct to try to build a personal relationship with one particular member of a corporate group, although such relationships may develop over time. 'You have to be really careful with personal relationships,' says Mike Inman of the Virgin Megastore in Tokyo. 'They are so important in Japan, but they can be abused by foreigners who tend to draw a firm line between work relationships and private relationships. Here in Japan, the two are intertwined.' To begin with, it is necessary to build trust between two groups: your company and .theirs. You need to create a new relationship, one that will bind your company into one small part of the Japanese commercial world and create the opportunity to move further inward as time passes.

The Japanese Language: Spoken, Written and Body

Japanese is a difficult language. It has some connection with the Altaic and Korean families of languages and, some say, a distant connection with both Finnish and Hungarian, but is totally different from most European languages in grammar, structure and vocabulary. What is more of a problem is that the writing system, based on Chinese characters, is not phonetic like ours, but symbolic. This makes it appear a very difficult language for a foreigner to learn.

The accepted truth is that, because all Japanese businessmen who are likely to deal with foreign companies speak some English, there is no need to speak Japanese to succeed in doing business in Japan. This is, like all generalisations, only partially true. Certainly, many very successful foreign businessmen have hardly been able to speak a word of Japanese, and many who were very fluent in the language have not been successful in business. It is also true that the basic requirements for business success in Japan are a thorough knowledge of your product range and the patience to carry through a plan over a long time span. However, it is equally certain that any knowledge of the language will help, and may give you the edge over your competitors.

One long-time resident of Tokyo, a successful member of the management team of a large British manufacturing company, has said on many occasions that although the Japanese language can take you some of the way towards understanding the ways of Japan,

you can never be Japanese. You are always a *gaijin*, so why bother
with the language? He believes that it would be better to spend the
time building relationships with Japanese clients than to spend hours
in conversation classes learning to say '*Konnichi wa*' (Good day) or
'*Domo arigato*' (Thank you). Bob Pearce of Cornes & Co. once
remarked (in English) to a Japanese department head (in a night-
club, building up relationships) that one of his English colleagues
spoke very good Japanese. The reply was withering: 'So does my 12-
year-old son.'

There is also the feeling among the foreign business community
that a *gaijin* who is too fluent in Japanese makes the Japanese uneasy.
Somehow they do not want foreigners to understand them too well.
'As your Japanese improves, people like you less,' was how Mike
Inman put it.

'I hear that a lot,' says Graham Harris of Lloyds Bank, a fluent
Japanese speaker, 'but I do not agree with it at all.' People do not
like you less, they just flatter you less because they know you are
beginning to tell the image from the reality. 'People who don't speak
Japanese see shadows where there are none. They think people are
talking behind their backs. Not speaking Japanese merely magnifies
the difficulties.' In his view, it is important to remember that the
English speakers among Japanese executives are not necessarily the
best businessmen. If you want to get your message across to the
people who really count in the hierarchy, you need to have some
grasp of Japanese, and the more you know, the better.

Japanese people never mind if we make mistakes in trying to
express our ideas in Japanese. 'Never be afraid of using the language,'
advises Chris Moss of Virgin Atlantic Airways. 'They will respect
you if you make an effort to learn. It is amazing how easy it is to
make yourself understood.' It is the person who never tries to speak
Japanese for fear of making a mistake who handicaps himself.

'I was shocked to find that so few top British businessmen in Tokyo
speak Japanese,' says Will Whitehorn, Virgin's Director of Corporate
Public Relations. 'We complain if the senior management of a
Japanese company in Britain is entirely Japanese, but in Japan not
only is the boss British, but people are there for years and don't speak
the language. I am pleased to learn that this attitude is changing
dramatically.'

Learning to speak Japanese is not an impossible task, although the
British, who are notoriously poor linguists, do seem to find it more

of a struggle than most. The spoken language has only a few basic sounds, a simple grammatical structure and very few irregular verbs. The vocabulary is entirely different from any European language, which means that it is difficult to work the British trick of pronouncing the English word in a foreign accent to get the meaning across. Although many words have come more recently into Japanese from outside, which makes things a little easier, distinguishing which ones have been borrowed and which are native Japanese is sometimes difficult.

Why should the word for 'telephone' be *denwa* (literally 'electric speak') while 'television' is *terebi*, an abbreviation of the English word? Can one recognise *wapuro* as an abbreviation of the English 'word processor'? Only with practice. Still, practice will make perfect, or something on the road to perfection.

It is still inevitable that most foreign businessmen will need an interpreter when they discuss business with their Japanese counterparts. This is not necessarily a disadvantage. Japanese is notoriously vague and it is very difficult for those who do not also have the cultural understanding of the way Japanese people think to deal only in that language. Interpreters serve a very useful function, and must be used if there is any prospect of a significant misunderstanding. Resident businessmen will use a member of their own staff to interpret, although there will also be many occasions on which the company you are dealing with will provide the interpreting skills. However, it is worth remembering, as Dr George Newns of British Telecom in Tokyo says, 'If you have a cultural interface, then the cultural problem should be with the supplier, not the customer. And that's all there is to it.'

If you are hoping to sell something to the Japanese, you must be able to do that in their language. If you are the buyer, you can insist on English, but if your company expects any success in selling to Japan, it must deal in Japanese.

Speaking no Japanese is never an advantage. There used to be stories of foreigners getting off minor brushes with the law through pretending not to speak the language, but although that was certainly true 20 years ago, it is not any more. 'I was stopped for going through a red light recently,' recalls Graham Harris of Lloyds, 'and the policeman said just one word to me. That one word was in English: "Licence." Now I suppose I could have pretended I don't speak English, but instead I handed over my licence. Nothing more was said. I had no chance to say I thought the light was still amber or to work out any other excuses, in English or in Japanese. He just wrote out the ticket and handed it silently to me.' You cannot get by if you do not speak the language.

The written language is something quite different. One of the reasons why it is so difficult to pick up Japanese without taking lessons is that it is not possible to read it without training. The Japanese writing system was imported from China, along with Buddhism, in the seventh and eighth centuries AD, but proved to be entirely unsuitable because of the lack of any similarity between Chinese and Japanese. However, Japanese is now stuck with the Chinese characters (*kanji*) and has had to develop its own systems of phonetic symbols (*kana*) to show verb endings, particles, prepositions and imported words for which there is no equivalent in Chinese. Each *kanji* has a meaning, but the pronunciation cannot be worked out from its shape. So if you walk down a street in Tokyo and see a bank, it is easy to tell that it is a bank because of the cash dispenser in the wall, because there are people going in, waiting patiently for 20 minutes or so while the paperwork is being handled on their simple transaction, and coming out again with little bank envelopes in their hands. But you will not be able to read the *kanji* on the door, which will tell you the Japanese for 'bank'. In France, under the same circumstances, you would be able to teach yourself automatically that the French for 'bank' is *banque*. The Japanese for 'bank' is actually *ginko*, but you will only learn that by taking lessons.

The written language is now a combination of *kanji* and the syllabic alphabets called *hiragana* and *katakana*. Each of the two syllabaries has 50 characters, each of which corresponds to a sound. There are five vowel sounds (a, i, u, e, o – all pronounced as short vowels as in 'cat', 'kit', 'cut', 'get', 'got'), which also have different *kana* when connected to each of nine different consonants (k, s, t, n, h, m, y, r, w) thus: *ka*, *ki*, *ku*, *ke*, *ko* or *ma*, *mi*, *mu*, *me*, *mo*, etc. There is also the final sound 'n'. All Japanese words end with a vowel or the 'n' sound. Learning the two *kana* syllabaries is not too difficult, and will be of tremendous help in getting about Japan if you are doing business there for any length of time.

Learning to write *kanji* is another matter. There are 1850 *Toyo Kanji*, an official selection of characters in which all newspapers are written, of which 881 'essential characters' must be mastered by the end of a Japanese schoolchild's sixth year of education. There are also a number of characters which are in common use in names, but not often seen elsewhere, and many thousand more which are used only rarely. Nelson's *Japanese-English Character Dictionary*, the best one for foreign students of Japanese, lists 5446 characters in its main body, of which the most complicated is a 48-stroke finger-twister which means 'dragons moving'. Japanese who were educated before and during the Second World War may be able to recognise well over 10 000 characters, although these days a well-educated Japanese will be fluent with only about 3000 characters.

There is no doubt that a knowledge of the written language helps considerably in getting about Japan, because not all road signs are written in *Romaji* (the Western alphabet) as well as in Japanese. It also helps in shops, when watching the news on television, when understanding the position of a businessman in the corporate organisation by reading his *meishi* (business card), and in ordering food at a restaurant. However, for a visitor to Japan, as opposed to a resident, the time taken trying to learn how to write Japanese could possibly be better spent planning, checking and rechecking the business aspects of the visit.

There are many ways to learn the language, either by a distance-learning system with tapes to play in the car, or at the many places within Britain where classes in business Japanese are available. In Japan there are boundless opportunities to learn Japanese, but it is always recommended that you do so through an established school, rather than through one of the many 'Japanese conversation teachers' who will come to your home and give what usually turns out to be a completely unstructured conversation class at which little is learnt. Many British and American housewives resident in Japan supplement their housekeeping by teaching English conversation with a similar lack of qualifications, but that is no reason why the same flawed principle should apply to learning Japanese. Speaking the language is always useful, and any words that you can learn and, much more importantly, use in Japan will be of immediate benefit in building a business relationship with any Japanese company.

The written and spoken languages are not the only ways of communicating with the Japanese. There is also body language. Japanese body language can identify the strength of relationships and the relative importance of a businessman in a team more effectively than his business card. It would be impossible to expound in full detail all the nuances of Japanese body language, but there are strong differences between the way a Japanese will move his body and the way a Westerner would under the same circumstances.

One of the most obvious points is the lack of eye contact which is the norm in Japan. In the West, a salesperson is taught to maintain direct contact in order to help conclude a sale, and the way a new job candidate maintains eye contact helps interviewers to decide whether he or she is suitable for the post that is on offer. In Japan, eye contact is rare, and if it is extended over any length of time it is an embarrassment. The sincere gaze into your opposite number's eyes should be avoided.

Possibly the most confusing aspect of Japan is the separation that the Japanese make between *tatemae* (face) and *honne* (the true voice). As one English colleague once remarked, 'With the Japanese, you always know where you aren't.' The late Lord Thorneycroft, when Chairman of the British Overseas Trade Board and chief negotiator with the Japanese for the British electronics industry, was once heard to remark, 'I am totally convinced that they are in fact Martians and the only solution is for them to go back there.'

The concept of saying one thing and meaning another is not unique to Japan. When asked to admire an elderly lady's hat, one does not necessarily tell the truth, and this concept is world-wide in its application. However, the Japanese will often take it a stage further, by never revealing the pretence, never telling even their spouse that the hat was awful. A favourite English phrase among the Japanese is 'frankly speaking'. When you hear that, you are looking at the mask rather than listening to their true feelings.

Within a group it is important that all members are seen to be equally committed to a decision, even if it is not actually true. But once a decision has been taken, it will be impossible to distinguish those who support it with their true voice (*honne*), rather than just with their face (*tatemae*). The Japanese, as a rule, tell foreigners the truth and nothing but the truth, but they do not necessarily tell the whole truth. That is where the gap between the voice and the heart is to be found.

The Sarariman *Lifestyle*

The image of the Japanese *sarariman* (businessman) as a 'workaholic living in a rabbit hutch', which is the description used by a European Community negotiator in the 1970s, is long past. It is true that the average Japanese male works 2100 hours a year, compared with

1871 hours in the United States and only 1575 hours a year in France, but this figure is rapidly decreasing, despite the labour shortage.

Their rabbit hutches are getting bigger too. Over 60 per cent of Japanese own their homes, about the same as in Britain but significantly more than in France (50 per cent) or Germany (40 per cent). Curiously, this percentage seems to be dropping. In 1987, for example, Ministry of Construction figures show that 88 700 new homes for rent were built, compared with only 56 300 for sale and 2300 company houses. Up to 1983, more newly built houses were bought than rented, but land prices have tended to take new home ownership out of the reach of the average Japanese *sarariman*.

On the brighter side, the average floor space in each newly built home is growing fast. It may be nothing more than a ferroconcrete condominium or apartment, but it will have just under 90 square metres of floor space, compared with 94 square metres in Germany and only 86 in France, according to Ministry of Construction figures. In America, of course, wide-open spaces still rule, with an average floor space of almost 150 square metres in each newly built home.

The average Japanese spends ¥16 000 each month on paying for his home, and a similar amount on utilities. This represents just over 10 per cent of his total monthly pay packet, which, by the end of the 1980s, had topped ¥300 000 per month (say, £22 500 per year). A further ¥31 000 per month is spent on 'transport and communications', which normally means the long commuter struggle. Residential land occupies only 4 per cent of the total land area of Japan, about one-seventh of the usable land area, but the population is becoming increasingly concentrated on the great cities. The result is that the price of centrally positioned real estate is well beyond the reach of the ordinary Japanese household, so it has become quite normal to commute for an hour and a half each day in order to fulfil the dream of the *sarariman*, 'a house with a yard'. Most homes built these days, whether houses, flats or condominiums, will have a combination of Japanese- and Western-style rooms inside. Shoes will be removed at the front door, and although the kitchen and possibly the dining room will be Western style, the bedrooms and living-room will almost certainly be *tatami*-mat rooms in the Japanese style.

A Japanese home is crowded. A family with two children may not have more than two bedrooms and one living-room, apart from kitchen and bathroom, so there is a great deal of pressure on space, and a huge premium is placed on harmony within the home. The old style of the father working late, arriving home after midnight and leaving for work again before dawn the next morning is beginning to die out, but the children's book about a father and child, *My Sunday Friend*, is still popular.

Commuting is unpleasant. The Japanese commuter railways tend to run on time and are not unduly expensive, but they are very crowded. Despite the fact that many private lines run alongside the state-owned JR (Japan Railways), there is never enough room during the rush hours. Twenty-eight million people live within 50 kilometres (31 miles) of the city centre of Tokyo (officially Nihombashi − the ancient bridge which marked the beginning, or the end, of the journey down the Tokaido road that linked the ancient town of Edo to the former capital, Kyoto). However, within that radius there are 2398 kilometres (1490 miles) of railway track and 1180 stations, so almost everybody lives within 10 minutes' walk of a station. Commuting by car is therefore not an option many people even consider. The crowding on the roads may not be as bad as inside the trains, but journeys are still much faster by rail. Each day, 2.9 million passengers use Shinjuku station, one of the main junctions between the rail and subway systems, and rush-hour crowding in the trains is now officially listed as '200 per cent to 240 per cent', compared with an average of 280 per cent in 1965. These percentages have, like everything in Japan, a detailed equivalent in the real world. According to the Tokyo Metropolitan Government definitions, 100 per cent is 'full to fixed capacity'. At 150 per cent, 'shoulders touch but you can still read a newspaper'. By 200 per cent, 'bodies are firmly pressed together but magazines can still be read' (it sounds like an Englishman making love), and at 250 per cent 'you cannot move your hands'. Three hundred per cent is 'physically almost impossible and dangerous', but if the average capacity is 240 per cent, there must still be many occasions when the physically almost impossible happens on Tokyo's commuter trains.

Tokyo's air is far cleaner than it was 20 years ago. Stringent exhaust-gas emission laws and environmental control laws governing factory pollution have turned what was once a frighteningly dirty city into one of the cleanest in the world. The same applies to Osaka and all the major conurbations in Japan. Living in Japan, working in Japan and raising children in Japan is a far more pleasant experience than living in many of the other big cities of the world. One thing that all Japanese cities seem to lack, and Tokyo in particular, is park space. Tokyo has only 3.4 square metres (36 square feet) of park for each of its residents, compared to New York's 19.2 square metres (206 square feet) or London's 30.4 square metres (327 square feet). There is also nowhere to park. Before you are permitted to buy a car in Japan, you must prove you have a parking space for it. It is not possible just to leave the car by the side of the road overnight, even if there are no double yellow lines in sight. Similarly, people rarely take a car with them when they go out for the evening, because they have no idea whether there will be anywhere for them to park. There is also a strict but simple drink-driving law, which sets a legal limit for alcohol in the blood of 0 ppm, so if you intend to drink at all you should not consider driving. Most Japanese who live in cities do not own a car. They have use of company cars during working hours if necessary, but otherwise they go everywhere by public transport.

Follow the Japanese lead on this. Use the public transport system to get about wherever you can. It is quick, cheap and simple to operate and, outside the rush hours, it is not overcrowded. 'You will be staggered by the efficiency, cleanliness and on-time service of the railways, and by the way they run the underground, which is absolutely spotless,' says Chris Moss of Virgin Atlantic. You will also avoid getting caught in a traffic jam, which happens all too often when you resort to using a taxi. Being late for an appointment is the ultimate sin, so make sure you have plenty of time to get to your destination, and go by public transport.

The biggest change in the lifestyle of the Japanese over the past 40 years has probably been in what they eat. Walk along any pavement in Japan and you will see 17-year-old boys well over 6 feet (1.8 metres) tall, strapping youths as big as their Western counterparts. The difference has been in the diet. Where once the Japanese ate mainly fish and vegetables, now there is much more red meat consumed. However, the Japanese diet is still healthier than the average Western one, with fewer calories per day consumed (2620 in Japan compared with around 3500 in western Europe and the United States) and a much lower percentage of animal fat than in any other advanced nation. The Japanese eat more vegetables than anybody except the Italians, more eggs and shellfish than any other nation, and consume barely one-quarter of the milk and dairy products that we do in Britain.

Breakfast is the only meal which has given way to the Western influence. A typical Japanese breakfast will now consist of ham and eggs, a slice of toast and a cup of coffee, just like in the West (except that the slice of toast will be an inch (2.5 centimetres) thick. The traditional breakfast consisting of rice, pickles and *miso* soup has lost popularity with the Japanese. It never gained any popularity with foreigners, which cannot be said of the rest of Japan's cuisine. There are so many different styles of food, all beautifully presented, that it would be impossible to detail them all here. However, they are all worth trying, from imported dishes like *sukiyaki* and *tempura* to traditional Japanese dishes like *sushi*, *oyako-don* or *udon*.

The Japanese housewife buys food every day. The Western concept of the once-weekly supermarket shop is still unusual. There are 45 food shops per 10 000 population in Japan, compared with 20 in Britain and only 10 in America, and the normal routine is to shop almost every day for the immediate needs of the household. The Japanese do not consume as much perishable food as the British or the French, so it is not particularly a matter of having to shop for food that must be consumed at once: it is just a social habit that continues. 'There are no medium sized stores in Japan,' notes Mike Inman of Virgin Megastores. 'There are the huge department stores and then the little corner shops, but in very few sectors is there anything in between.'

Education

In 1872, one of the first acts of the new Meiji government was to set up a national education system. The 1890 Imperial Rescript on Education is one of the best-known documents of modern Japanese history. It hung next to the emperor's portrait in all schools in Japan and was the foundation for moral teaching for over 50 years. Its views were mainly Confucian, 'Be filial to your parents, affectionate to your brothers and sisters,' and it also urged the people to 'pursue learning and cultivate arts, and thereby develop intellectual faculties and perfect moral powers.'

In 1947, the educational system was revamped under the American Occupation. Children must now have nine years of compulsory education and, like the American system, these years are divided into elementary (*shogakko*), junior-high (*chugakko*) and high schools (*kotogakko*). The vast majority of schools are in the public sector, and all schools follow an identical timetable. Formal lessons begin at the age of six, when all children begin their elementary education. By the age of 12 they are expected to have gained basic literacy and numeracy skills: no straightforward task with the extremely difficult Japanese written language. At the age of 12, children go on to their middle school, and at the age of 15, they sit exams that largely determine the course of their future lives.

During these three years, many children will also attend a private cramming school, or *juku*, in order to ensure that they pass these crucial exams well. They often stay at school until 10 or 11 o'clock at night, and enjoy far shorter holidays than their European or American counterparts. It is a terrible pressure to put on young children, but it does not finish at 15, when legally they can leave school. Of over 2 million junior-high-school graduates each year in the late 1980s and 1990s, about 95 per cent stayed at school.

High schools are either academic or vocational. The academic schools prepare pupils for university, and pressure to get into the right university is intense. There are 499 universities in Japan, and they are (very unofficially) ranked according to their perceived prestige. A graduate of the great national universities, the University of Tokyo (*Todai*) and Kyoto University (*Kyodai*), or of the leading private universities like Keio and Waseda, will be able to pick his career in government or the business world. Students who make it to universities lower down the pecking order will have a tougher time. Suicide is still comparatively common among students who failed to reach the university of their choice.

Life for the university student is wonderful. After 12 years of intense pressure, there is really nothing to do at university unless you really want to. Many students spend their university years forming relationships that will stand them in good stead in the future and in perfecting their sporting or drinking skills, but few bother with doing any work. One British lecturer at Yokohama University felt he had to fail one of his English students who had not turned up to a single lecture all year. He was told by his head of faculty that he could not do so. 'I was told just to give him the lowest pass grade, so I did.'

Employers now know that university life is little more than a well-earned rest, so their human resources staff see their role as bringing the new graduate employee back to the level of hard work

and commitment he had in high school. The high school can therefore be as important as the university in helping a company decide
whether a graduate is suitable. Graduates' high-school records can
determine whether they know how to work. If they do, they go
back into high-pressure Japanese society, with its threat of *karoshi*,
death from overwork, a fate that never seems to befall university
students.

The Silver Age

In 1992 there were 16 million Japanese over the age of 65, which is
13.1 per cent of the population. This group is defined by the Nikkei
Research Institute as the 'Silver Agers', and by the year 2025 they
will comprise one-quarter of the Japanese population. The nation is
ageing rapidly, and the enormous growth in the number of healthy
and increasingly long-lived 'Silver Agers' represents a challenge to
the Japanese economy and to potential suppliers to this age group.

The average assets of the over-60s was estimated in 1987 to be
¥11.5 million (say, £72,000) excluding real estate. Eighty-two per
cent of the over-60s are homeowners, as compared with 60 per cent
in the population as a whole. They are wealthy and like to save
their money, partly because they cannot think of much they want
to spend it on. In the past parents used to live with their children
and grandchildren, but the pressure on space in the cities has made
this less and less practical, and the older people are beginning to
develop their own lifestyles independently of their children.

Japan is a country where age is revered. September 15 is a national holiday, Respect for the Aged Day. Business and government
leaders are often still active in their seventies and even their eighties:
Prime Minister Murayama was 70 when he took over in 1994.
However, 38 per cent of firms still set their retirement age below 60,
and staff who are not wanted by their companies beyond that age
find themselves looking at twenty years of retirement unless they
can find another job. This they usually do. Work remains the most
popular pastime for the over-60s, with many of the 5.2 million
workers in their sixties working on into their seventies. Many stay
on as company advisers or are self-employed, but because staying
active is often more important than money, some retired people are
willing to take positions far less exalted than the jobs they have left.
A recent government survey showed that three-quarters of 'Silver
Agers' were satisfied with their lot in life, a percentage that rose to
88 per cent when asked of the women only.

CHAPTER 3

THE WORK ETHIC

Management Practices and the Employment System

'Some Japanese people say to me, "This foreign company is more Japanese than my own",' says Mike Barrett of GKR Japan. 'It is the foreign companies that are the museums of Japanese management practices.' His view is that many foreign companies in Japan perpetuate their own myths about what Japanese management styles are, and the short-term expatriate managers dare not rock the boat. 'Good management practice is good management practice anywhere. There are cultural differences between the UK and Germany and the UK and France, just as there are between the UK and Japan. The myths of Japanese management culture are based in reality, but Japan has moved on. What we are doing now is fighting clichés, demolishing myths and destroying icons. The myths are either out of date or else based on the differences between Japanese and American practice, not the European practice, which is much closer to the Japanese.'

To understand the way that Japanese companies operate, and the way that individuals within those companies work, we must keep in mind the network of relationships upon which Japanese society is based. The work ethic is imbued into the Japanese because they are part of an organic whole which will not function properly unless all parts of that whole are working well. They work for the good of the group rather than for their own personal advancement because they have been taught that the good of the group, whether it be a company, a government ministry or a baseball team, is their own personal goal. 'I read a report which said that the most important words to the Japanese are "effort", "persistence" and "thank you," says Helen Guinness, managing director of Four By Four Consultancy, the management training and cross-cultural business experts. 'The favourite words of Europeans were "love", "family" and "fun". One set of ideals is not superior to the other. They are just different.'

'The trouble with this country,' says Tim Bridgman of Swire, 'is that it is so difficult to make any sensible generalisations.'

'The Japanese' is a dangerous generalisation. The citizens of Japan range from the livestock farmers in the north of Hokkaido to the pineapple and sweet potato growers in Okinawa; from the highly sophisticated international businessmen of Tokyo and their more cynical colleagues in Osaka to corner-shop traders in country towns and villages; from university professors at Kyoto University to first-grade schoolchildren in Shikoku; and from 200 kilogram (31 stone) sumo wrestlers to the thousands of little old ladies whose frail bodies belie their inner strength. (Differences in the market and business styles of Tokyo and Osaka are studied in more detail in Chapter Seven.) Nevertheless, 'the Japanese' are a more homogenous society than almost any other in the world, and using the generalisation, while always dangerous, is probably more apt than with any other nationality. The Japanese often use the phrase '*Wareware Nihonjin wa*' (we Japanese) to preface an outrageous statement, so they themselves, at least, believe in the generality. 'The most important factor about the Japanese consumer,' says Hiromi Yoshida of Dentsu, 'is their homogeneity. In Britain social class divides taste. In America it is race and geography, but there are no such differences in Japan. There is more individuality than there used to be here, but Japanese consumers still follow major trends together.'

It is possible to criticise the Japanese for not being 'efficient' in Western terms, but not for not working hard. 'The difference between Japanese and European business,' says Ben Thorne, 'is that the Japanese try to prevent problems from happening, while we look for problems to solve.' Western 'efficiency' does not take human relationships into account, nor social obligations. It is a digital attack on a set of problems requiring solution. The Japanese version of efficiency is more painstaking, more thorough and more concerned with the implications of actions. The Japanese may spend much longer than Western businessmen worrying over the right solution to a problem, and in the majority of cases the answer they would each come up with would be the same. Just occasionally, though, the Japanese method of trying out every possible way of solving the problem, however odd it may appear at first, will come up with a better answer. Japanese answers will certainly always have taken into account the potential effect on other people and organisations, so they will be in a far better position to react when those effects occur. Western businessmen often seem surprised by the impact of their actions on the community. Their Japanese counterparts are rarely surprised by reactions their decisions provoke within Japan, although they are still on occasion caught out by foreign responses to what they propose.

The basic values of Japanese society, the homogeneity, the community spirit and the feeling that personal aggrandisement is not the right goal to aim for, are all reflected in the Japanese work ethic. People still work long hours and for no extra reward other than the knowledge that they are a worthwhile member of the group. The system has been described as 'Confucian Communism', a strange but successful combination of Confucian ideals of obedience and respect for one's elders with the communist ideals of 'to each according to his needs, from each according to his abilities'. Japanese society is highly capitalist in its understanding of the virtues of a market economy, in its competitiveness and its ability to think of the customer first, but it is unique in the way that this does not override the collective structure that runs the economy. The Japanese use the words 'we' and 'us' much more than the words 'I' and 'me'.

Lifetime employment is perceived by outsiders as the way that Japanese corporations run their staffing policy, and in Osaka they are proud of their claim to be the origin of this style of management. The Sumitomo and Konoike family merchant companies of the eighteenth and nineteenth centuries stipulated lifetime employment for their employees, a strict system of seniority, apprenticeship, the importance of workers' harmony and consensus decision-making, but this paternalistic style has changed considerably since feudal times ended in the 1860s. It is certainly true that within the largest companies the normal way of recruiting is to take on people only once a year upon graduation and train them in the ways of the company, so that by the time they have been working for 10 to 15 years they are highly motivated and productive members of the team. The majority of graduates are also still looking for that type of career structure, but this is not the whole story. It never was.

Even within the largest manufacturing companies, there have always been a large number of workers who are only part-time. Closer investigation reveals that these are not just office cleaners and security guards: it is common that many of the production line staff are officially employed on a part-time basis, or through an agency, so that they are not true members of the company. When the stories of lifetime employment and no redundancies are repeated, almost as an article of faith, the non-believer is allowed to remember that these tales apply only to the full-time employees, and that the 'casual' element on a corporation's payroll is not protected in the same way. 'Lifetime employment is a convention rather than a set of rules,' says Mike Barrett. He believes that, 'It really only started in the years after the war, and was in some part imposed by the American-style labour laws.' The fact that the retirement age can be set as low as 55 in some companies also gives lifetime employers the chance to get rid of the less productive members of their teams after a comparatively short 'lifetime'. All the same, the accepted norm is for lifetime employment for anybody who wants to stay, and a company will do everything in its power, even in the bad times, to protect its staff.

The story (possibly apocryphal) of Mitsubishi Heavy Industries in the early 1970s is a classic of this paternalistic type of management concern for employees. The slump in the shipbuilding industry brought on by the first oil shock created problems for the company, the largest of the big shipbuilding firms, as well as for all its rivals. However, at roughly the same time, the motor manufacturing arm of MHI, which subsequently became Mitsubishi Motors, was experiencing a rapid growth in its business. MHI is reported to have solved the problem of how to keep its shipbuilding labour force usefully employed by transferring several thousand people, virtually overnight, from building ships to building cars. The two plants were not particularly close, so it involved a geographical disruption as well as a change in skills for many people. This was seen at that time as the right solution to the problem. However, with the labour shortage that now exists in Japan, there is no doubt that the work-force is less keen to be herded by management into any field they consider appropriate.

The Japanese Corporation

Japanese corporate structure tells us a great deal about the way Japanese business works, and the way a Western businessman needs to act to fit in with his Japanese counterpart. From first principles, the attitudes and directions of Japanese corporations are different from those of most Western nations.

If a British company had to make an important decision involving several million pounds, the board would have three sets of influences to consider. They would have to assess the reaction to their decision of their shareholders, their customers and their employees. They might also have to take into account the views of their bank but, in general terms, bank borrowings in Britain are a less significant part of corporate finance than they are in Japan. To a British board of directors, the general order of importance of these different human elements is shareholders first, workers second, customers third. In some cases one could say that it is shareholders first, second and third, and the rest nowhere. Any decision which involves a major outlay of shareholders' funds must have the full backing of the shareholders.

In Japan the situation would be almost the exact opposite. '*Kyaku-sama wa osama*' means 'the customer is king', and in any Japanese business the most important group of people is the customers. That is one reason why the Japanese have such a reputation for detailed market research, and why many of their greatest successes have been in general consumer goods. They think of the customer first. This applies to directors deciding where to put a factory as much as to marketing departments deciding on the colour of a packet of soup. Second in importance are the employees, who are treated as the vital cog in the overall long-term success of the enterprise. If the staff are not happy and well-motivated, the operation cannot work and the products will not sell. It sounds like a succession of trite corporate platitudes to say that we think of our customers and our staff first – the sort of blurb in an annual report that cynics would laugh at – but in Japan these ideas are not only taken seriously, they are the daily guiding ideals of management and workers alike. Finally, a long way behind in the considerations of the board, comes the shareholder. The shareholder and the bank are often one and the same, so the bank is informed and takes a close interest in what is going on. But all shareholders in Japan are also customers, and they realise that unless the products being sold by their company are popular there will be no dividend, no share options and, eventually, no company. Japanese banks are allowed to own up to 5 per cent of the stock of any company they also have business dealings with, but the influence of a shareholder bank is much greater than 5 per cent. In Chapter Four, the relationship between industry and its sources of finance is explored more fully.

The hierarchy of Japanese corporations is at first sight quite similar to that of any business concern anywhere in the world. They have presidents, chairmen and managing directors, as well as department chiefs and export sales managers, and all these titles are translated into English on their business cards. A diagrammatic representation of a corporate structure in Japan would look very much like that of

Japanese Business Titles

JAPANESE TITLE	ENGLISH TITLE	ROLE
Kaicho	Chairman of the Board	Usually non-executive, but may be executive.
Shacho	President	Similar to ...
Daihyo Torishimariyaku	Representative director	The director who has power to represent the company legally: the holder of the corporate seal.
Senmu	Senior managing director	There may be more than one *senmu* in a company. It is the next rank below *shacho*.
Jomu	Managing director	The rank below *senmu*.
Kansayaku	Auditor	Unlike a Western auditor, this is not an accounting position. The auditor is the 'ombudsman' on the company board, to see that the shareholders, staff and customers are fairly treated.
Bucho	Department head	The top functional rank below *jomu*.
Jicho	Deputy department head	
Kacho	Section head	
Kakaricho	Chief or supervisor	
Shain	Employee	

Combinations of these titles are routine. The head of the Sales Administration Department (*gyomubu*) of a large company, for example, who is also a representative director of the company, will be called *daihyo torishimariyaku gyomubucho*. There may be several representative directors in the company, all of whom are legally empowered to sign on behalf of the company. There is only ever one *shacho* or *kaicho*. The title '*dairi*' may appear after a rank, showing that the executive in question is a deputy or assistant.

a British corporation. A Westerner can feel confident that he is finding his way around the Japanese company, and seeking out the real decision-makers, if all he does is go by what is written down for him. As always in Japan, appearances are deceptive.

Japanese business titles vary very little from company to company, but in Japan rank does not define the task carried out, as it does in the West. The principle of gaining rank by age and length of service as well as by skill and results is still very firmly entrenched, and respect for one's elders is a firm part of every company philosophy, just as it is of Japanese society itself. However, Japanese companies very rarely have explicit job descriptions and, for example, a section head (*kacho*) might carry out many of the functions of his superior or his junior, if that was how the department needed to operate. Japanese corporations do not give their employees a specialised career path; they are expected to take a flexible attitude to the tasks they are required to perform. 'The Japanese are a nation of corporate specialists,' says Helen Guinness. Mike Barrett would agree: 'On the job market, experienced managers with the broad approach are available, but not so many with specific skills.'

A paper published in the late 1980s identified one of the main differences between Western and Japanese management systems as being the fact that in the West there is intense pressure on an individual's current performance, while in Japan there is little or no pressure on individual performance, as that is subordinated in the performance of the group. The theory was that the Japanese emphasis on co-ordination and co-operation rather than on efficiency and results means that the pressure on individual managers is less. But Mike Barrett disagrees. 'The pressures on executives are enormous,' he says. 'There is a great deal of individual competition for promotion. Not everybody goes all the way up in the elevator. Some get off at the lower floors.' Even in Japan, the individual is valued for his personal contribution, and it is identified within the contribution of the team.

Styles of Management

The Japanese say that there are three styles of management which can work, and they are summed up in the styles of the three great feudal leaders of the sixteenth and seventeenth centuries: Oda Nobunaga, Toyotomi Hideyoshi and Tokugawa Ieyasu. For almost 200 years, until the late sixteenth century, Japan had been plunged in civil wars and the ambition of Nobunaga (1534–82) was to bring all Japan under one sword, as he put it. The sword, of course, would be his. He was an ill-tempered and treacherous man who was not concerned for convention, but he was also a brilliant military leader. When he was murdered by one of his own retainers, Hideyoshi (1536–98) took his place. Hideyoshi was a poor peasant who had risen to the top through his own determination and military skills, but he had a reputation for magnanimity which was in complete contrast to that of Nobunaga, and which contributed as much to his success as did his military power. His name 'Toyotomi' was one which he took for himself, and it means 'bestower of wealth'. He used persuasion and compromise rather than extermination as a means of getting his way. Tokugawa Ieyasu (1542–1616) was less impetuous than Nobunaga and less colourful than Hideyoshi, but he had greater foresight and greater political skill. His eventual triumph led to 250 years of rule by the Tokugawa family, the longest period of political stability in Japanese history.

The story goes that the three great leaders were one day resting by a tree, and they noticed a bird which was not singing. Nobunaga at once said, 'If the bird does not sing, I will kill it.' Management by threats and decisive ruthlessness is unusual in Japan today. Hideyoshi looked up and said, 'I will make it sing.' Just as a bird is meant to sing, so a manager must ensure that his staff do what they are trained to do. Hideyoshi's complete confidence in his own ability to make the bird sing is also in many ways typical of the way Japanese management teams assume that any problem is surmountable, if they apply themselves to it. Ieyasu's methods were more cautious: 'Wait, and the bird will sing.' A bird or a man will always eventually do what it is in his nature to do. Patience is the overriding virtue. It is Ieyasu's philosophy which is most often followed in Japan today.

A very commonly used word in Japan is *gambare*, which is most usually translated as 'Don't give up' or 'Do your best'. It is a standard term of encouragement heard at school, at sports events and in company meeting-rooms. Never give up, have patience, persistence and do your best: all these ideas are encapsulated in the one word *gambare*.

There is a school of thought that says that major Japanese corporations have no middle management at all. The Western top-down style of management, with decisions filtering down the corporate structure to the operational level, and the Japanese from the bottom up style of management are frequently contrasted. Certainly, employees who hold the title of manager do not really manage in the Western sense of the word. Many people who are nominally the leaders of a department or section may be among the weakest members of the team. Because decisions are made by the group, their job is not necessarily to make sure that their views win the day, but rather to ensure that the views which do win the day are put into action with unanimity and eagerness.

Consensus and Decision-making: **Nemawashi** *and the* **Ringi** *System*

The way the Japanese take decisions has often been pin-pointed as the single major difference between Japanese and Western business methods. In a way this is true, but only because the decision is a visible sign of progress, and is therefore more obvious than other aspects of business practice. If we understand the system of relationships within Japanese society and Japanese business, and the paternalistic nature of most Japanese corporations, then the decision-making process is one that even a *gaijin* should be able to understand.

There are two main features of the decision-making process in Japan, which can be best described in the two Japanese words *nemawashi* and *ringi*. *Nemawashi*, as we have already seen in Chapter One, means 'binding the roots', and comes to mean 'thorough preparation'. This ought to be blindingly obvious to every businessman in any nation: before you make a major decision you need to check the facts, see what the opinion within the company is, and look at the effect your decision will have on the other operations of the company and its competitors. However, what happens all too frequently in the West is that a senior manager makes a decision unilaterally, and expects to impose it upon those below who will have to carry it out. A decision to sell hundreds of thousands of pounds' worth of sand to Saudi Arabia can be made in an instant, if a manager wants to make it, but it will never be put into effect unless his subordinates understand and support the thinking behind it. An instantaneous decision can result in months of total inaction until the opposition to the idea is either defeated or, in the worse but more usual case, destroys the original decision. The Nobunaga style of threats can be effective to a limited extent, even in Britain, but almost every British businessman can think of an example of a management edict that never worked. Few of his counterparts in Japan would be able to come up with similar stories.

Nemawashi is more than just checking that nobody opposes your decision before you announce it. Western businessmen prefer to have a solution to test for acceptability before they hold discussions about any problem. In Japan, there is no feeling that there ought to be a solution before the real problem has been identified. The analogue Japanese mind, which realises that every detail of business life is part of a whole and affects every other part, expects compromise to be the best answer. The digital Western mind believes that a perfect solution can be found.

The formal *nemawashi* process within a Japanese company involves all interested parties. A series of meetings will be initiated by the department in which the potential problem has arisen, to learn the views of everyone who might be affected by a new decision. If, for example, a British company has proposed that a Japanese manufacturer of hi-fi equipment act as sales agent for their range of speakers, the decision whether or not to do so would not be left merely to the sales department. The new range of speakers, if it was to be handled, would affect the working lives of the accounts department, who would have to provide the finance, process the invoices and pay the supplier; it would affect the sales department, and the marketing department who would have to decide how best to reach the market for the new imported range; it would affect the production department, who would have to decide whether the imported speakers threatened their own range of goods and whether they could become involved in some sort of local manufacture; it would affect the sales administration department; it might affect the research and development team, who would be able to look firsthand at the way a foreign company had tried to solve problems of manufacture and design that they also had been struggling with; it would affect the distribution and warehousing operation; and it would affect the human resources department. All these groups must be given a chance to comment on the idea, or to ask questions about it. No directorial decree will override the need to have lower management committed to a project before it is given the go-ahead. The lead in this consultative process would be taken by the sales department, assuming that was where the initial contact was made, but in leading the discussions they would not be seen to be putting forward any specific proposals.

What happens is that within the company there are a number of meetings, either between just two departments or, more generally, across several disciplines, at which the main points of the idea are investigated. This will result in some matters being settled and some new questions being raised. The new questions require answers, which means contacting the British company again. For a foreign company trying to come to an agreement with a Japanese one, the length of time involved in the negotiation tells you nothing. It is the number and reasonableness of the questions which give the clue as to how the discussions are progressing.

The Japanese are not good at saying 'no'. Although there are words in their language which are translated as 'yes' and 'no', there is no true equivalent for either idea. It is seen as unforgivably rude to say 'no' to anybody, particularly somebody who has taken so much trouble to come to Japan to present a set of proposals, so the message has to be conveyed without any ill will. If, during the process of *nemawashi*, a number of impossible questions are raised, that is the Japanese way of saying 'no'. For example, if the British speaker-manufacturer had clearly stated from the outset that his company could supply speakers in oak, pine and beech, and in no other woods, but the Japanese kept asking for mahogany speakers, that should be construed as meaning the Japanese do not want to do business. Even if the British company decided it must do everything to keep the discussions going, and agreed to a range of mahogany speakers, the Japanese would probably quickly come up with another unanswerable objection as their way of saying 'no'. The material the speakers are actually made in is of little importance: the true reason might be that the Japanese would have to close down a line in their factory, or that agreeing to the deal would create a problem with one of their distributors who already handles a competitive line. The British company may never find out the real reason, but it needs to recognise a 'no' when it hears one.

The word that Japanese-English dictionaries say means 'yes' is *hai*. This word (pronounced 'high') does not really mean 'yes' at all. It means, 'I have heard and understood what you said. I am now thinking of a suitable reply.' In many circumstances, *hai* equates with 'yes'. 'Is it raining?' '*Hai*' (Yes, it is raining cats and dogs). But if the question is, 'Will you buy 10 000 widgets at £10 each?' the answer '*Hai*' would not mean 'Yes'. It is not a cue to rush back to your hotel to fax the joyous news of your first big order back to head office. It simply means, 'I heard what you said and am thinking of a way to let you down easily. Maybe I will ask if you have any mahogany widgets.' The best refusal I ever came across was proudly related by an export manager on the flight back from his first trip to Japan: 'They told me our products are too good for the Japanese market.' No product is ever too good for the Japanese market. Japan demands quality as a matter of course. Anybody who is told that his products are too good is being told gently that there is no possibility of business, but for an unstated reason. Anybody who believes his products are too good for the Japanese market is too naïve for his own good.

By the end of the *nemawashi* process, which may take weeks or even months, a solution emerges as generally the most widely acceptable view. This does not necessarily involve compromise. It involves one view emerging as the right answer, usually a view that has been subtly championed by one man or one section who feel strongly that it is the correct decision.

The decision, once reached, will be formalised by the *ringi* system. *Ringi* means 'a document which goes round'. The *ringi* system consists essentially of a written proposal prepared by the initiating department and circulated vertically and horizontally to all those who have been concerned in the consultation process. Because of the preparatory *nemawashi* that will have preceded the circulation of the *ringi* document, it is unlikely that there will be any opposition to the proposal. Equally, it is unlikely that the proposal will be exactly as originally conceived by the initiator. The document has to be stamped with the personal seal of all recipient department managers (rank, rather than any considerations of who is most involved in the decision, determines who puts his seal on the document), and this circulation and stamping process can take some time. However, once the decision has been approved and the *ringi* has returned, fully signed, to the originating department, it is possible for the company to move very quickly indeed. In simple terms, this confirms the accepted view of the contrast between the Japanese company which takes a long time to make a decision, but then moves rapidly towards the goal; and the Western company whose manager may take a decision very quickly, but fail to energise his staff into turning his vision into reality.

Any foreign businessman who has been involved from the outside in the Japanese decision-making process will talk of how much time it all takes, and how it appears for many months that absolutely nothing is happening. There is no reason, of course, why he should not get in touch with his Japanese contact while the decision-making process is going on. It must always be remembered, though, that no reply at all is one more Japanese way of saying 'no', and further unwanted contact may only serve to prolong a wasteful process even further. But as Malcolm Carlisle of Smiths Industries Medical Systems says, 'You can't overestimate the amount of time a Japanese corporation takes to be comfortable with change.' In a culture where they always take the long-term view, there is caution about change without very careful consideration.

Yet Gordon Williams, recently British Consul-General in Osaka, believes that 'what one notices about Japan is the speed of change. One example is the speed at which Sony moved into public broadcasting equipment when the consumer market looked saturated.' There is no real conflict of views here. Once the *nemawashi* has been completed and the *ringi* circulated and approved, there is a dazzling speed of subsequent action, based on the fact that everybody involved in the action is already fully committed to the decision upon which it is based. So Sony may have been considering the public broadcasting equipment market for some time before making any announcement to the outside world, but once it had made its decision, it was able to move with great speed and purpose. Once a Japanese company is comfortable with the change it is proposing, it is no longer comfortable with the present state of affairs, and new ideas should be introduced as quickly as possible.

Many foreign companies have been caught out by this apparent split between the very slow and the very fast. Companies who during the negotiating process quoted ambitious delivery times find themselves with the obligation to meet schedules that they had no expectation would come to pass. Companies who have said product modifications were possible have been forced to make extremely rapid changes in their Japanese lines when go-ahead decisions have been taken. It never pays to exaggerate your company's abilities during a long-drawn-out negotiation because it is almost certain that you will be asked to perform to the best of those abilities. If your company is selling products to Japan, then the Japanese client is the customer and the customer is king in Japan. You are his servant. He will expect his royal due.

This is incidentally one reason why products for the Japanese market often differ from those on general sale in other parts of the world, and why a product adapted for Japan is often relaunched on the world market with spectacular success. A lot of work has gone into the decision about the product specification and market in Japan, and the end result is often an improvement on what is offered elsewhere. If a product can sell in Japan, it will almost certainly find a market in other parts of the world. The Japan specification, which might at first have been greeted with expressions of horror, can often become the standard world-wide specification. The Japanese want the best and usually know what that is. If your company is unwilling to provide it, you will have to learn how to understand the word 'no' without it being spoken.

The Role of Women at Work in Japan

Japan is, of course, a man's country. Business has traditionally been run as a man's club, and the highest ambition for a woman has been to marry a *sarariman* and bear his 2.3 children. However, as with everything else in Japan, things are certainly beginning to change.

There is now a labour shortage and, whereas until the early 1980s the pressure was on women to achieve the goal of 'being properly married', as Ms Noriko Hama, now Chief Representative of Mitsubishi Research Institute in London describes it, nowadays there is a strong need to have women, especially qualified women, in the work-force. As a result, it is becoming much more normal for women to think of their jobs as careers rather than opportunities to find a husband. The labour shortage was one of the driving forces behind the passage of the 1985 Equal Employment Opportunity Law, which requires employers to give equal opportunities to women in terms of recruitment, salary and career progression. Before its enactment, women were 'protected' by a law which forbade them from working very much overtime, and which set a level of fines for employers who forced their female staff to work over-long hours. This actually had the effect of holding women back rather than protecting them. The Ministry of Labour was very strict in enforcing the law, and often prosecuted companies which over-used their female employees. What actually happened was that the women worked long hours, but pretended they did not. Their employers also pretended they did not and, of course, paid no overtime as part of the pretence.

'In 1975, when I joined MRI,' says Noriko Hama, 'we would be quite shocked to come across a woman still working for a company after five years. They were usually married and gone after three years. At that time, being a woman and being new to the company,

I had to be the first person at the office each morning to turn the lights on. It was not part of my duties, but it would have been quite scandalous if anybody else had done it for me. Then I got out a cloth and cleaned and tidied all the desks. I would even sharpen people's pencils for them, in that age before personal computers and tiny calculators. I would do this even for the men of equal rank to me, and all this would be done before anybody else arrived. Then I would be involved in *ochakumi*, serving out the Japanese tea to everybody as they arrived. That would take me up to 10 o'clock each morning, probably. If you wanted to be perceived as a committed female, you had to go through this ritual rigorously.

'You could not rebel, or you could not hope to further your career. That ambition – to have a career – had to be hidden deep inside you. The mask of the obedient female employee had to be in place for a long time, perhaps three years, before you could breathe a word about career development.'

By 1991, 81.8 per cent of female university students who graduated in the spring found jobs, compared with 81.1 per cent of the male graduates. For the first time ever, a higher percentage of women graduates found jobs than men, but this was in part explained by the fact that in 1994, for every 100 male graduates there were 141 jobs advertised, while for every 100 female graduates there were only 61 suitable jobs. So many female graduates still have to take jobs which are well below their qualification levels. Before the 1985 Act companies tended to employ women either on production lines (in which case they were often employed only as part-time employees or contract employees through an agency) or as decorative additions to office life. This meant that the younger and prettier they were the more likely they were to get a job. 'The more highly educated you were,' remembers Noriko Hama, 'inevitably the older you were and the more difficult it was to find a job. If you had a master's degree, potential employers would turn pale. If you had a PhD, nobody wanted you at all.'

The Equal Employment Opportunity Act now guarantees equal pay for men and women at all levels of the management hierarchy. However, as a recent survey showed that only 1.2 per cent of managerial jobs at department-head level or above were held by women, it is difficult to show that the Act is being enforced. The same survey showed that only 13 per cent of businesses, one in eight, even hoped to have more women as department heads one day, and barely one third of companies were looking to increase the numer of women in middle management. Only 52 per cent of Japanese companies are even looking to put women on to the lowest rungs of the management ladder, so there is a long way to go before women are taken for granted in the Japanese business hierarchy. In 1994 over 80 per cent of all female graduates in work were employed as secretaries.

Most Japanese women in business are grouped under the category of 'OL', which is Japlish for 'office lady'. The image of the OL is that of an elegant, unmarried lady in her twenties or possibly early thirties with, most important, a great deal of disposable income. The young, uncommitted women of Japan have a great deal of money to spend on foreign travel, fashion, consumer durables and entertainment, and they do spend it. Saving money is not as popular as it was among their parents' generation, and the OLs like to spend. Nowhere in the world will you see so many elegantly and expensively dressed young women as in the big cities of Japan. 'Women are the biggest consumers,' says Nobufumi Kurita of JETRO in London, 'and men are working for women to consume goods.' But they no longer leave work promptly and obediently upon marriage, despite this selfless desire of the Japanese married man to work to fill his wife's purse. A survey for the Sumitomo Bank recently showed that about 80 per cent of young housewives did not want their lives to be only housework and child raising (which leaves the astonishing total of 20 per cent who *did* want nothing more than washing up and changing nappies), while one in eight of those questioned said that she would not give up her job even if her husband insisted. The career woman is beginning to take hold in Japan. Husbands, on the other hand, see things through a different set of spectacles. Three-quarters of all married men in their thirties, surveyed for the Daiichi Kangyo Bank, thought that women had become very powerful, and 48 per cent said women do not hesitate to say what they think. Despite this, three men in four said they would not mind women holding managerial positions if they had the ability.

The accepted view within Japan is that they are entering a new era of social and business structures. Everything that used to work, from 1945 until the late 1980s, is now starting to look uncertain, and a new approach to the problems facing Japan in the next century is required. The Japanese education system, one institution that shows little sign of change, tends to produce articulate and well-structured minds but also tends to stifle initiative and original thinking. The new approach could well come from women, with a different sense of priorities.

'The environment of business in Japan is changing for women,' believes Nobufumi Kurita. 'Japanese companies are trying to promote women to high-level positions.' 'I have been working in a man's world for twenty years, and I do not feel at any disadvantage now,' says Mie Teno, Managing Director of Deltapoint Management Consultants in Tokyo, and for many years the person who headed the drive to attract Japanese inward investment to Telford. 'There are no longer any uncomfortable situations, even though when I talk to *kacho* or *bucho*, they are all men. They are all men because it takes twenty years or more with the same company to reach these ranks, and women are maybe not patient enough.' 'The male business community's view of the company as something to live and die for cannot contribute much to adjusting Japan to the new economic environment,' says Noriko Hama. Women are less committed to the company than to their own professional goals, so an increasing number of women in key positions may well have the effect of changing the paternalistic style of most big Japanese corporations. The promotional route within the bigger Japanese companies, which follows a zig-zag path through many different disciplines, may well be affected by an increase in the numbers of women in the management pool, for Japanese women have a greater professional commitment than Japanese men. They want to be specialists rather than corporate generalists, which is the traditional role of the Japanese manager.

The search for the 'woman's angle' will not help if, once this obscure angle is found, it is departmentalised, type-cast or made the basis of a ghetto mentality. Posts open to women in typical Japanese corporations are usually restricted to a few areas such as public relations, product development or personnel. They are powerful in the arts, in publishing and in fashion, and increasingly so in some financial services, but you will not find many in senior posts in NKK, Toyota or the civil service. The setting up of women-only research teams, for example, has become quite common on the assumption that the female point of view is helpful in developing new ideas. 'Let's put all the women together and let them chat happily' seems to be the prevailing attitude of male management looking for solutions. Women-only think tanks, female creative advertising teams and women-only market research teams are more likely to lead to new prejudices and new constraints, despite the image in a successful television advertisement of a young woman who hums the tune 'Freedom of choice of occupation' as she goes about her working day.

The foreign woman doing business in Japan has her own set of problems. 'Japanese men feel some shyness when facing foreign ladies,' says Kurita. '"How can I talk to her?" "I'm afraid she is looking at me and judging my poor English harshly" are their thoughts. This prevents normal communication.' Ms Hama goes further. 'Japanese men are terrified by foreign female executives. That's the best way to put it. They are tongue-tied and bewildered.' She nevertheless believes that they take to foreign women in business more readily than to Japanese women.

Rosemary Yates, director of Japan Advisory Services Ltd, and a regular business visitor to Japan, does not take such an apocalyptic view. 'I am treated as an honorary man,' she says. 'I am rung up at the crack of dawn. I am expected to find my own way around Tokyo. I am taken out to *karaoke* bars with porno videos. I have never been to Soapland (the generic name for brothels thinly disguised as bath and massage parlours), but otherwise I find no problems.' Yates speaks fluent Japanese, which obviously helps her to be treated as an honorary man – or, perhaps more important, as an honorary Japanese – but as she says, 'All foreigners are an exception to normal Japanese business rules, so although a woman may be treated with misgivings at first, in the long run she will do well or badly according to her own skills.' Two of the most successful British consumer businesses to come to Japan in recent years are the Body Shop and Laura Ashley, both founded by women. However, all other things being equal, a foreign man is more likely to be acceptable to the Japanese business community than a foreign woman.

CHAPTER 4

THE STRUCTURE OF JAPANESE INDUSTRY

Japan Inc.

'When you look at the relationship between government and business in Japan, you have really got to start from the premise that they are one and the same thing.' That is the view of Ben Thorne who, as a former Commercial Counsellor at the British Embassy and now a consultant on Japan trade, has considerable experience over many years of both sides of the partnership. 'You will hear a lot of trite remarks about the homogeneity of the Japanese, but this is because they use consensus to seek agreement, rather than confrontation. They eliminate the "them and us" syndrome. All Japanese feel they are on the same side. Foreigners complain about Japanese bureaucracy, but what they are really complaining about is its efficiency.'

In Thorne's opinion, the education system is what makes it easy for the Japanese to understand each other. 'Government and business interlock. They are run by people who know and trust each other. They knew each other at school, at university, and these early relationships can go all the way back to what village you come from.'

A bureaucrat is highly educated, an elitist closer to the French model than the British one, although, as Mike Barrett of GKR says, 'The Japanese corporate structure is exactly like the British Civil Service. They even have a *ringi* system in the Civil Service, and *nemawashi*.' Everything a Japanese bureaucrat does is done for the good of the country. In the same way that, in Japanese industry, bold mission statements intended to focus all employees on one corporate goal are to be found on posters and placards all around the corporate premises, so that the worker never forgets the wood for the trees, in the Japanese Civil Service the good of the country is always the mission.

This has in the past led to the old stereotype of Japan Inc. – the belief that all Japanese businessmen are thinking first of their country and that no single foreigner could hope to breach this monolith. Ben Thorne says that this no longer exists. 'The Japanese are merely trying to protect their own interests rather than meaning to upset others. They are often misunderstood, but I believe this is changing. They are getting better and better as internationalists. Remember, they have only been at it for a little over 100 years. They are fast learners. Their basic motive is still to get the best for Japan and their organisation, but this also means not being quite so blinkered about the effect of their actions on other people.'

The links between Japanese government and industry are sometimes closer than just friendly meetings and mutual assistance. In Japan, there is a peculiar but well-established practice called *amakudari*. *Amakudari* literally means 'descending from heaven', and it is the word used to describe the recruitment of senior government civil servants into industry, once they reach the government retirement age. Almost every major Japanese company will have on its board, either as an executive director or as a non-executive adviser, somebody who once held a senior position in the 'right' ministry. For example, a major construction firm will have on its board an ex-under secretary from the Construction Ministry, while an electronics company will have recruited somebody from the Ministry of Posts and Telecommunications, from the Ministry of International Trade and Industry (MITI) or perhaps even from the Defence Agency. For the civil servants, the system of *amakudari* gives them an opportunity to earn good money after a lifetime of governmental pay scales, while from the company side, hiring such an august member of the government establishment gives access to the inner workings of the ministries with whom it has to deal most closely. It is, as one British businessman with considerable experience of Japan and many other foreign countries describes it, 'a racket'. But it continues, and is unlikely to change in the foreseeable future. It helps Japanese businesses get closer to their bureaucracy, but it penalises foreign companies in Japan, most of whom are unable to attract civil servants looking for a descent from heaven.

The extent of *amakudari* sometimes surprises foreign businessmen. A Japanese research company, Toyo Keizai Shimpo-sha, calculated that of almost 2000 companies listed on the Tokyo Stock Exchange in 1989, around 4 per cent of their representative directors (*daihyo torishimariyaku* – the ones with the real power) came from government offices or public corporations. In total, there were 1000 ex-government officials on the boards of publicly quoted companies at the time of the survey.

The official links between government and industry are through organisations such as the Keidanren, usually described as the Japanese equivalent of the British CBI. Although the CBI holds regular meetings with the Keidanren (full name: *Keizai Dantai Rengo-kai* – Federation of Economic Organisations), there the similarity ends. The Keidanren has enormous power. 'It's not like the CBI, it's more like the KGB,' says Ben Thorne. The Keidanren was established in 1948 and is described as a 'private non-profit economic organisation which maintains close contact with trade associations and corporations at home and abroad.' It is made up of over 120 trade associations and almost 1000 leading corporations and its official purpose is to work out practical solutions to domestic and international economic problems through co-operation with foreign countries. A rather coy understatement makes it clear that 'the Keidanren sometimes transmits its unified views to the Government and the Diet, as well as to interested political parties.' The use of the word 'sometimes' is superfluous. The Keidanren holds great power within Japan, which it uses regularly, and is undoubtedly the operations room of the Japanese business world.

There are other important private industrial organisations, including the Keizai Doyukai (Japan Association of Corporate Executives), a forum for individual corporate businessmen, whose aims are to promote the sound development of the Japanese economy, to enhance the nation's welfare and to build a well-balanced society. The Nikkeiren (full name: *Nihon Keieisha Dantai Renmei* – Japan Federation of Employers' Associations) concerns itself mainly with labour-management relations, but from the employers' point of view. It transmits its policy decisions on wages and working conditions to the government agencies concerned. These decisions have the authority of firm proposals, of which the government takes close note. The Japan Chamber of Commerce and Industry (*Nihon Shoko Kaigisho*) consists of about 500 local chambers of commerce and has a more powerful say in industrial policy matters than most of its Western counterparts, the French Chamber of Commerce always excepted. Below the big and powerful groups, the smaller organisations, to the tiniest representative body, slot into the hierarchy. All interlock and exchange views. The object is wherever possible to obtain consensus.

The Japanese respect authority, and large groups seeking to promote the welfare of a particular sector of society are natural figures of authority, worthy of respect. The government is the largest of these groups and is worthy of a great deal of respect. The Japanese do not, as a general rule, like to oppose policies or statements made by government, as that would be denying it the respect it is due. The Japanese government does not like making statements which would excite opposition, because that implies that the consensus agreement system has broken down. 'The only time they run round like headless chickens,' says Ben Thorne, 'is when consensus evades them.'

Administrative Guidance

Japan's bureaucracy works through the system of 'administrative guidance' (*gyosei shido*). This involves giving advice which is not usually written down, so that if the advice proves wrong, unworkable or unnecessary, there is no comeback. 'The company did it of its own accord,' is the usual ministry response to an action taken in the wake of administrative guidance. This style of operation is necessary because most Japanese control is exercised on the basis of 'inclusive approval' rather than the more common international theory of 'exclusive approval'. In other words, the Japanese authorities would have an 'approved list' for a particular category, and anything not on that list is automatically banned. Most Western bureaucracies rely on a 'banned list', so that anything not on the list is automatically approved. The Western method makes it easier to introduce new ideas and concepts; the Japanese method makes for time-wasting at best and deliberate obstruction at worst. However, it can also be shown that the Japanese method forces manufacturers to be sure their products or services are entirely safe and acceptable in a way that the more open Western method might not. Once again, we see the analogue Japanese mind looking for ways of relating new concepts to existing ones, opposed to the Western style of being less concerned about the effect a new idea may have on the *status quo*.

A good example of the effects of the Japanese system can be seen in the workings of the Pharmaceutical Affairs Law, which was established partly with the object of keeping narcotics out of Japan. Now it is changing towards the purpose of promoting the health of the nation. However, there is still a list of acceptable medical materials and devices which defines what can be sold and used in Japan. As medical science advances, the Pharmaceutical Affairs Law seems to get in the way of the health of the people, rather than promoting it, and effectively keeps the smaller companies out of the game. A Japanese importer of medical devices told me, 'These days, registration of a new product with the Ministry of Health and Welfare takes about three months from the date of submission. Any question raised by the ministry means we have to start again. Usually the problems concern the materials. In one case, we had to disclose the percentages of the individual elemental constituents in a metal framework, even though the manufacturer himself did not know this. But it is no good replying, "This is confidential," because the ministry will not let us conceal this information. The FDA registration documents in the United States were of no use either. So we had to install test equipment in a new laboratory to do the analysis over here. To do work on any medical device, we have to have a manufacturer's licence, even though we only want to be an importer. All this raises the stakes of participation very greatly.'

Things are beginning to change, but the ministry, if asked, would have said that there was no written law which applied to this case and that the importer had of his own free will applied for a manufacturer's licence and built a laboratory. There would be no mention of the administrative guidance which persuaded the importer that this was the only way round his problem.

The practice of law provides another example of administrative guidance. There are several discriminatory factors in the way that foreign lawyers are able to practise in Japan. In contrast, Japanese lawyers are allowed much more freedom when working abroad, and we can assume that American and European pressure on Japan to reciprocate will eventually bring results. But at present not only are foreign-qualified lawyers not allowed to give legal opinions in Japan, they are also not allowed to give their practices the same names that they have overseas. This is because law firms are generally partnerships and not legally incorporated companies. Partnerships can only be named after the partners resident in Japan. So Linklaters & Paines, for example, one of the biggest British commercial law practices, has to be known as Grundy Gray in Tokyo. Partner Tony Grundy explains, 'We have to have all our headed notepaper and so on in the name of Grundy Gray rather than Linklaters & Paines, which is a nuisance as we have to change all the notepaper when one of the partners moves on. It also confuses Western businessmen with whom we communicate, because they thought they were dealing with Linklaters & Paines, not Grundy Gray.' The partnership sought advice and were told that the particular regulation concerning the name of the practice could probably be flouted, in fact if not in spirit. 'So we have Grundy Gray in Japanese on our notepaper and Linklaters & Paines in English, which seems to keep everyone happy.' Administrative guidance found the compromise, but if ever the strategy was considered unacceptable, there would be no record of anybody ever having suggested otherwise.

For most foreign businessmen, the most important ministries are the Ministry of Finance (*Okura-sho*) and the Ministry of International Trade and Industry (MITI or *Tsusan-sho*). Whatever the nature of your business, it is probable that at some stage your company will come into contact with one or other of these two monoliths. The best advice is not to fight it. There will be a mountain of paperwork, meetings and questions to be suffered through, but in the end the only right solution is to remember the Japanese virtues of patience and persistence, and trust to victory in the end. Swimming against the flow does not work. Remember the Japanese proverb, 'The nail that sticks up gets hammered down.'

All this makes Japan sound like a highly regulated market-place, where all the cards are marked in favour of the dealer and where initiative is dead. This is absolutely not the case. The Japanese government has always believed in a flourishing and highly competitive home market as the basis for international success. 'I know of no other market-place in the world where competition is as strong as it is in Japan,' says Helen Guinness of UKOA. The government, by using administrative guidance to encourage companies to set their sights on particular targets, usually within a narrow product spectrum, has created the appearance to the outside world of Japanese domination across the industrial board.

The Structure of the Keiretsu

Keiretsu does not have an exact translation into English, but it is used to describe the large economic groupings of Japanese corporations, intertwined with cross-shareholdings and mutual goals. Before the Second World War, these groups were known as *zaibatsu*, but the Occupation forces decided that their structure was a major contributory factor in Japan's ability to arm itself so effectively, and abolished them. They made holding companies illegal, hoping, in this way, to eliminate the vast corporate groups which could effectively manage sections of the economy and the populace as they wished. The effect of this regulation was not what had been expected. The *zaibatsu* continued to operate, in fact if not in name, by building stronger ties of cross-shareholdings, even though there was no one parent company and no one president guiding all the companies. The revisions of 1949 and 1953 in the American-inspired anti-monopoly laws helped in bringing the old *zaibatsu* back together, although one of the pre-war big four, Yasuda, never quite re-emerged in its old shape. In many ways, the new structure suits the Japanese style even more than the old style. The *keiretsu* are locked together in relationships both financial and personal, extraordinarily powerful as a group but with no clear leader – a microcosm (or more properly, a macrocosm) of Japanese politics, of Japanese families, of Japanese schools and universities, and of the Japanese way of life.

There are two types of *keiretsu*, as defined by the standard work on the subject, *Industrial Groupings In Japan* (published and updated every other year by Dodwell Marketing Consultants). There are horizontal groupings (see p. 69) and vertical groupings (see p. 67). It is the horizontal groupings, the true successors of the *zaibatsu*, that are most often identified with the structure of Japanese industry.

Dodwell describe six major horizontal *keiretsu*. Three of them (Mitsubishi, Mitsui and Sumitomo) originate from the old *zaibatsu* and three groups (Fuyo, DKB and Sanwa) consist of companies that have splintered from the medium-sized *zaibatsu* of old and now cluster around three major banks. (The Fuyo group, based around the Fuji bank, is virtually the successor to the pre-war Yasuda *zaibatsu*). These six are known as *Rokudai Kigyo Shudan*, the Six Major Industrial Groups. The groups contain companies which participate in all the major sectors of Japanese economic life, from manufacturing to insurance, from transport to real estate, and, most importantly, from banking to trading. All the groups are kept together by a spider's web of cross-held shares (see Table 3 overleaf), by presidential councils which unofficially, but nevertheless firmly, control and decide group policy, by joint investment by group companies in new industries, and by intra-group financing by the group's banks.

Cross-shareholding serves not only to bind a group without a parent together, it also protects each company within the group from take-over threats. No contested take-over bid has succeeded in Japan for many years, and indeed, Professor Shinobu Muramatsu of the Department of Economics at Seikei University, Chairman of the Mergers and Acquisitions Sub-Committee of the *Nihon Kogyo Shinko Kyokai* (Japan Industrial Progress Association), a MITI-sponsored body, believes there will never be a successful one. 'A contested take-over implies there is no consensus, so even if it would be successful, it could not work.' The cross-shareholding is a defence against the mechanics of a take-over bid through the stock market. The Japanese need for consensus is the ultimate protection against a corporate raider.

Table 3
Cross-shareholding Ratios of the *Rokudai Kigyo Shudan*

Group	1985 (%)	1987 (%)	1989 (%)
Mitsubishi	20.4	21.9	21.6
Sumitomo	22.2	21.3	20.5
Fuyo	16.7	17.5	16.7
Mitsui	17.6	17.8	14.3
Sanwa	14.2	13.9	14.1
Daiichi Kangyo	15.6	15.4	13.8

Cross-shareholding ratios are calculated as the percentage of total shares held by group companies ranked in the top 10 shareholders of each company, to the total paid-up capital of the collected group companies listed on the Tokyo Stock Exchange.

(Source: Dodwell Marketing Consultants)

Japanese banks are allowed by law to own up to 5 per cent of the shares of a client company. For example, the Mitsubishi bank owns 5 per cent of Mitsubishi Corporation, the trading arm of the group, and 3.6 per cent of Mitsubishi Heavy Industries. However, as MHI owns 3.2 per cent of Mitsubishi Corporation, and 3 per cent of the Mitsubishi Bank, and Mitsubishi Corporation owns 1.7 per cent of its bank and 1.6 per cent of MHI, it is already hard to tell exactly what percentage of which company is owned by whom. Given that the Mitsubishi group consists of over 170 companies, all with a little bit of each other, it is quite impossible to calculate where the ultimate shareholding power lies. The Mitsubishi group is entirely typical of the way the *keiretsu* work.

The key companies in most of the *keiretsu* are the banks and the trading companies. The huge Japanese general traders, *sogo shosha*, have taken on a significance of their own in the Japanese economy, and they certainly do not limit their activities merely to buying and selling on behalf of their group members, although that has always been at the heart of their business. The general trading companies invest also in new markets, at home and abroad, extend business credit and act as matchmakers for business partnerships. All of the nine biggest general trading firms have close links with the *keiretsu*. These nine companies (C. Itoh, Kanematsu Gosho, Marubeni, Mitsubishi Corp., Mitsui & Co., Nichimen, Nissho Iwai, Sumitomo Corp. and Toyo Menka) have a combined annual turnover above ¥100 000 billion (almost $800 billion). The largest single trading company is C. Itoh. It is a member of the DKB group but also has strong historical links into the Sumitomo group, showing that affiliation to one group does not exclude co-operation with others.

The importance of the *keiretsu* to the Japanese economy and to Japan's whole business life cannot be over-stated. They employ over 5 per cent of the total work-force, and represent a staggering one-quarter of the paid-up capital of all Japanese companies. Their total annual sales are one-sixth of the total sales of Japan, and their net incomes slightly better than that, at 17.2 per cent of the country's total net income. Without their unique brand of bringing in business and profits to Japan, the economy would not have been able to forge ahead so successfully after the Second World War, and Japan would not be anywhere near the economic and industrial power that it is today. This provokes two reactions in the West: to try to beat them, or join them.

The structure of the *keiretsu*, having no equivalent in the West, is inevitably described as unfair by some sections of Western governments. In that it is a reflection of Japanese society, it could certainly be described as unfair by those trying to impose Western rules on the game. '*Keiretsu* trading is so much talked about these days,' says Andy Andoh of Dodwell, 'and the American government in particular is putting so much pressure on Japan, that we may soon see some reverse discrimination.' All the same, he does not see any reduction in the importance of the *keiretsu* in the foreseeable future. Bob Pearce of Cornes & Co., a Western-owned Japan trading company, believes the *keiretsu* trading houses are starting to find it tough. 'There has been tremendous political pressure on importing, which led MITI to go to the big trading houses and tell them they would be judged on the amount they imported. So the trading houses signed up everybody under the sun, but in most cases did absolutely nothing about it. You would do better to look for the specialists.'

Fighting the *keiretsu* may be possible with government help, but to win in Japan requires consensus, not coercion, so the line more often taken by foreign companies is to use the *keiretsu* companies for their own purposes. 'It does matter getting into the Big Six. You can trade or have other business relationships with more than one group,' says Andoh, so you won't open one door and see five more shut. However, if, for example, Mitsubishi are your company's sole agent, it is obvious you will have better access to Mitsubishi group companies than to other groupings. 'If you are closely associated with one of the *keiretsu*, with a joint venture or licence agreements, for example,' says Andoh, avoiding the use of the word 'no', 'your ability to access the other groups will be rather limited.'

However, breaking into a market where there are already existing relationships has always been difficult in Japan. 'We once offered Mitsui a 0.75 per cent discount on their import costs by virtue of our being able to plug into Bank of Japan finance,' says Graham Harris of Lloyds Bank, 'but Mitsui said no. They said they would go on using the Taiyo Kobe Mitsui Bank, despite the fact that Mitsui's net trading profit was minimal and we were offering them 0.75 per cent off their finance costs. The reason they gave me was that the Taiyo Kobe Mitsui Bank was not doing well at the moment, and they could not desert them. One of my colleagues said that this represents a non-tariff barrier, just what the Americans are always talking about. Yes, I suppose it is, but I can't get too worked up about it.' Lloyds Bank is still very successful in Japan. 'Non-tariff barriers are where you look for them,' Harris believes. 'If you do not want to see them, they won't be in your way.' The Japanese unwillingness to change partners is not merely because of the *keiretsu* links. Any existing supplier/customer relationship is hard to break into, because the two companies feel an obligation to each other that goes beyond the mere economics of the deal. Having a link into a *keiretsu* company can often be an advantage, but it is by no means an open sesame to the Japanese market.

The Japanese economy has seen the emergence over the past two decades of a new type of *keiretsu*, the vertically integrated group, as opposed to the historical type of horizontally integrated group. As

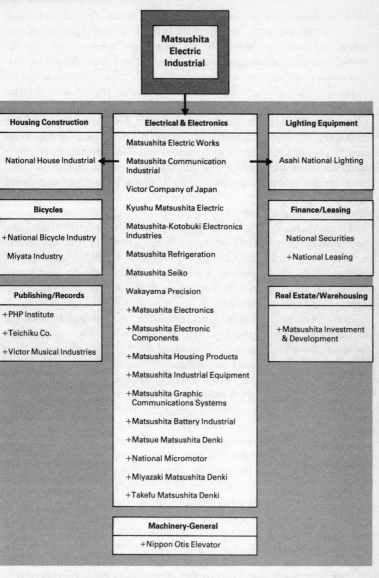

The Matsushita Group
A Vertically Integrated Keiretsu

Matsushita Electric Industrial

Housing Construction

National House Industrial

Electrical & Electronics

Matsushita Electric Works

Matsushita Communication Industrial

Victor Company of Japan

Kyushu Matsushita Electric

Matsushita-Kotobuki Electronics Industries

Matsushita Refrigeration

Matsushita Seiko

Wakayama Precision

+Matsushita Electronics

+Matsushita Electronic Components

+Matsushita Housing Products

+Matsushita Industrial Equipment

+Matsushita Graphic Communications Systems

+Matsushita Battery Industrial

+Matsue Matsushita Denki

+National Micromotor

+Miyazaki Matsushita Denki

+Takefu Matsushita Denki

Lighting Equipment

Asahi National Lighting

Finance/Leasing

National Securities

+National Leasing

Real Estate/Warehousing

+Matsushita Investment & Development

Bicycles

+National Bicycle Industry

Miyata Industry

Publishing/Records

+PHP Institute

+Teichiku Co.

+Victor Musical Industries

Machinery-General

+Nippon Otis Elevator

Parent Co. → Subsidiaries or affiliates

+   Unlisted companies

(Source: Dodwell Marketing Consultants)

we have seen, in the horizontally integrated groups there is no overall parent company, and the group's activities spread right across the economic spectrum. Vertically integrated *keiretsu* are groups of companies within one industry, linked by subsidiary and affiliate bonds. Typical examples are Toyota, Nissan, Toshiba, Matsushita and Nippon Steel. The groups consist of a major parent and a large number of subsidiaries or affiliates who would normally act as supplier, distributor or, occasionally, financier for the parent. So, for example, Matsushita Electric Industrial is the 'parent' of the Matsushita group, and its member companies include companies working within a comparatively narrow product framework, mainly in electrical and electronics goods. There is also a real estate company, which develops property almost exclusively for the Matsushita group, and finance and leasing companies.

These vertically integrated groups tend to have fairly close links with one or other of the horizontally integrated *keiretsu*, and Matsushita is typical in this. The Sumitomo group holds about 13 per cent of Matsushita's shares, and directors from both the Sumitomo Bank and Sumitomo Life Insurance have served on Matsushita Electric Industrial's board.

Some vertically integrated groups are now being established within the horizontally integrated groups, and this is creating some friction between the members of the horizontal *keiretsu*. It could be said that the horizontal groupings are voluntary associations of companies sharing the same goal, while vertical groupings are compulsory associations of companies sharing the same parent. We can choose our friends, but not our families, as the rather pessimistic Western saying has it.

Mitsubishi Heavy Industries, while still one of the three leading members of the Mitsubishi group, and a member of its *Kinyo-kai* (presidential council), is also the leading company in a vertically integrated group of its own which includes Mitsubishi Motors. MHI have their own real estate companies and trading companies, and as long as these remain comparatively small and specialised it is unlikely that there will be any serious friction with other companies following similar businesses within the Mitsubishi horizontal *keiretsu*. But as time passes and the individual companies follow their opportunities as they arise, there is an ever-greater chance of internal conflict which even the presidential council will not be able to resolve entirely. If two companies within the same group want to compete within the

The Mitsubishi Group
A Horizontally Integrated Keiretsu

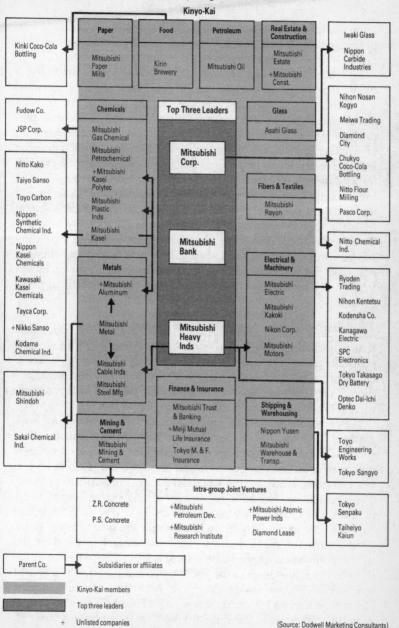

Kinyo-Kai

Paper	Food	Petroleum	Real Estate & Construction
Mitsubishi Paper Mills	Kirin Brewery	Mitsubishi Oil	Mitsubishi Estate / +Mitsubishi Const.

Kinki Coco-Cola Bottling

Iwaki Glass — Nippon Carbide Industries

Fudow Co. / JSP Corp.

Chemicals
Mitsubishi Gas Chemical
Mitsubishi Petrochemical
+Mitsubishi Kasei Polytec
Mitsubishi Plastic Inds
Mitsubishi Kasei

Top Three Leaders

Glass
Asahi Glass

Nihon Nosan Kogyo
Meiwa Trading
Diamond City
Chukyo Coco-Cola Bottling
Nitto Flour Milling
Pasco Corp.

Nitto Kako
Taiyo Sanso
Toyo Carbon
Nippon Synthetic Chemical Ind.
Nippon Kasei Chemicals
Kawasaki Kasei Chemicals
Tayca Corp.
+Nikko Sanso
Kodama Chemical Ind.

Mitsubishi Corp.

Fibers & Textiles
Mitsubishi Rayon

Nitto Chemical Ind.

Metals
+Mitsubishi Aluminum
Mitsubishi Metal
Mitsubishi Cable Inds
Mitsubishi Steel Mfg

Mitsubishi Bank

Electrical & Machinery
Mitsubishi Electric
Mitsubishi Kakoki
Nikon Corp.
Mitsubishi Motors

Mitsubishi Heavy Inds

Ryoden Trading
Nihon Kentetsu
Kodensha Co.
Kanagawa Electric
SPC Electronics
Tokyo Takasago Dry Battery
Optec Daí-Ichi Denko

Mitsubishi Shindoh

Sakai Chemical Ind.

Finance & Insurance
Mitsubishi Trust & Banking
+Meiji Mutual Life Insurance
Tokyo M. & F. Insurance

Shipping & Warehousing
Nippon Yusen
Mitsubishi Warehouse & Transp.

Mining & Cement
Mitsubishi Mining & Cement

Toyo Engineering Works
Tokyo Sangyo

Z.R. Concrete
P.S. Concrete

Intra-group Joint Ventures
+Mitsubishi Petroleum Dev.
+Mitsubishi Research Institute
+Mitsubishi Atomic Power Inds
Diamond Lease

Tokyo Senpaku
Taiheiyo Kaiun

Parent Co.	→	Subsidiaries or affiliates

Kinyo-Kai members

Top three leaders

+ Unlisted companies

(Source: Dodwell Marketing Consultants)

same market-place, either the dictates of the market will decide who prevails or, more likely, the power of the *keiretsu* will make the decision first.

Professor Yoichiro Murakami of the University of Tokyo has a theory that the world is a household: 'Sometimes the Earth is called a spaceship, and sometimes a village, but the Earth is not artificial like a spaceship, nor is it a village, which conveys a flavour of pre-modernity in the use of the word. The world is a complicated mixture of artificial and natural, of modernity and pre-modernity.' Japan, he feels, values the ideals of the household in that it looks for integration, for a solution to problems not in the best form but in a less conflicting form. 'Housekeeping does not assume the existence of the unique or the optimum solution to a problem. There are cases where several mutually exclusive alternatives should be simultaneously adopted. To be and (not 'or') not to be, that is the question.' That is how the *keiretsu* work. They are and they are not; they do and they do not; they can and they cannot. There is no perfect answer, only a relationship to be built or maintained, but, if at all possible, never broken.

The Profit Motive and Market Share

It was once suggested by a British businessman in Japan that he originally thought he was running in a mile race against his Japanese competitors, but realised too late that they were running the Marathon. The Japanese, as we have seen, take the long view; an early success is not always a good sign.

James Abegglen and George Stalk Jr, in their standard work *Kaisha – The Japanese Corporation* (Harper & Row, 1985), state that 'low profitability of Japanese companies and their access to seemingly unlimited sources of borrowed funds, are commonly held to be two key competitive advantages not available to Western competitors.' The problem is that nobody agrees on how success ought to be measured, or what is the goal of a limited company. In Europe and America, the answer would usually be that the goal is profit and a good return for the shareholders on the capital invested in the business. In Japan, as we have already seen in Chapter Three, the shareholder is low down in the pecking order of who ought to benefit from the success of a business enterprise. Many Japanese corporations gauge their success by market share, or perhaps by return on capital invested, rather than the standard Western percentage return on sales. Japanese banks, who are of course shareholders as well as money-lenders, look for a strong long-term position among their clients rather than a current trading profit, and lend money vigorously on this basis.

Twenty years ago, major Japanese corporations had the most remarkable (to Western eyes) debt:equity ratios as borrowings appeared to outstrip shareholders' funds by a massive amount. Over the past decade, as the policy of aiming for market share has brought in the profits that the banks hoped it would, borrowings have decreased rapidly. It is no longer true to say that high levels of debt are a characteristic of Japanese corporations, nor that companies operate on profit margins that would be totally unacceptable in the West. It can be said that Japanese companies could still build up bank debts at comparatively low interest rates, in a way that would not be possible in the West, always assuming the bank is convinced of the long-term viability of the business. However, business bankruptcies have consistently run at higher levels than in the West, partly because the Japanese are not afraid to try and fail and then try again. But there is no magic safety net waiting to break the fall of those who get it wrong.

These high debt ratios have in the past helped Japanese companies to compete internationally in a way that we might categorise as 'unfair' because Japan did not have the same banking laws as us. It is an interesting footnote that for many of the Japanese export boom years of the late 1970s and 1980s, some foreign banks in Japan were not authorised by their head offices to lend money, even to major Japanese corporations, because the balance sheets did not fit in with the tight Western banking criteria of 'a good risk'.

The Unions

One further example of the uneven playing field in Japanese corporate structure is the union system. After the Second World War Japanese labour relations were at a very low ebb, with frequent strikes in almost every sector of industry. It took a strike at Nissan in 1953 to settle matters in favour of the management (and, they would say, consensus decisions) once and for all. The national Car Workers' Union, the *Zenji-roren*, called an indefinite strike at Nissan, but the company was prepared for it. By working with the employers' organisation, Nikkeiren, they arranged bank loans to cover the period of the strike. More astonishingly, they got an agreement from all their rivals, including Toyota, not to poach their market share while the struggle, seen as one for the good of all motor manufacturers, lasted. At the same time, Nissan established its own company union, with the slogan, 'Those who truly love their union love their company.' Nissan won the strike after many weeks, and it marked the beginning of the end for industry-wide trade unions in Japan. The Nissan model now became the norm: company unions sprang up everywhere, and workers set about loving their union and their company in equal doses.

The company union is a perfect example of consensus, of relationships, of successful housekeeping. The management cannot be too tough in dealing with its union or it will demoralise its work-force and begin a downward spiral of confidence, quality and profitability. On the union side, there is no point in coming out on strike, or even threatening to, unless the situation is too desperate for there to be any hope of a negotiated solution, because the only people who will be harmed are the company members. As the work-force in Japan still enjoys, for the most part, a lifelong relationship with one company, it follows that harming that company will harm the workers for life. This creates a degree of co-operation within Japanese industry which would be virtually unthinkable in the West. The idea of 'them and us', which is the main pillar of British industrial relations, is almost non-existent in Japan. Everyone starts as part of the union, and until they reach a senior management level they remain, equally, loyal union members and loyal company employees. Perhaps this is another non-tariff barrier, but it is not one that can be got rid of; it is part of the Japanese character.

CHAPTER 5

EXPORTING TO JAPAN

Preparing for Your Visit

Japan is a long way to travel, and to make the journey with less than complete preparation will be a waste of time and money. There are a number of simple tasks that should be done by everybody preparing for a business trip to Japan, whether it is their first trip or their umpteenth one.

Visas are not a problem for the visiting British passport holder. There is no need to apply in advance; on arrival in Japan you will be granted a temporary visitor status visa, lasting 90 days, which is long enough for practically all business trips. If you want to stay in Japan and work, you must apply to the Japanese Embassy consular section well in advance of your proposed trip. The normal processing time for a working visa is around three months, but as there are so many variations on visa requirements for people intending to stay in Japan, it is best that you contact the Japanese Embassy direct. They will give all the help required. You are not allowed to earn money in Japan without the correct visa, and such is the efficiency of the immigration system that it is difficult to get away with trying to do so without the correct formalities. It is absolutely not to be recommended.

Hotel bookings should also be made in advance. There are many hotels in both Tokyo and Osaka, but the most widely used international ones get very full, despite the high prices of their rooms and services. There is no doubt that the best hotels in Tokyo compare with the best anywhere in the world, and business visitors invariably comment on the joys of their hotel. However, there are more than just the five-star international chain hotels available for the visiting businessman. If the biggest names are full when you want to visit Japan, rooms will almost certainly be available in other hotels which may be less luxurious but no less suitable for a business stay. A word of warning should be given about bookings at certain times of the year. In September and October especially, and whenever there is a major international trade fair, the pressure on hotel rooms is intense.

You must always be sure that your booking has been confirmed before you get there: there will not be room for anyone who turns up with a hopeful smile but no confirmation slip.

Timing your visit is important. Make sure you do not arrive at a time which coincides with national holidays (see below), or at the Obon season (around August 15), when it seems the entire population goes back to its home town to visit relatives and remember ancestors. Holidays are fixed on particular days – not Mondays or Fridays as is common in the West – and almost never disrupt the rest of the working week. The exception to this rule is that from 29 April (the late emperor's birthday, celebrated as 'Greenery Day' since his death) until 5 May (Children's Day), the Japanese celebrate what is known as Golden Week. Any business visits that are timed for then will be bound to fail.

Japanese National Holidays

1 January	New Year's Day
15 January	Coming of Age Day
11 February	National Foundation Day
20/21 March	Spring Equinox
29 April	Greenery Day
3 May	Constitution Day
5 May	Children's Day
15 September	Respect for the Aged Day
23/24 September	Autumn Equinox Day
10 October	Physical Education Day
3 November	Culture Day
23 November	Labour Day
23 December	Emperor's Birthday

(The late emperor's birthday, 29 April, has been renamed 'Greenery Day', but remains a national holiday. 'Golden Week', between 29 April and 5 May, is a time when few businesses work normally.)

Always plan your itinerary in detail before you arrive. Your appointments should be made and confirmed well in advance of your arrival, and you should not necessarily expect that new meetings can be set up during your visit. It may be possible to do so, of course, but nobody visiting Japan on business should arrive with an empty diary and hope to fill it up by means of a few telephone calls. Do not expect to fit in too many meetings each day. It is difficult to give a hard and fast rule about how many can be arranged for each day, but you should probably allow at least one hour each, even for basic courtesy meetings in your hotel. For visits to company premises, it is probably wisest to allow half a day for each. At a meeting you should not just sit back and follow the Japanese timetable: if you appear not to have any pressing engagements, a Japanese host will do his best to fill the time he thinks you have vacant, so you need to create some slight feeling of urgency in all your appointments. However, do not expect to rush in to a company headquarters, sit down and complete your business and rush out again, all in a few minutes. This is not only un-realistic but also displays a lack of courtesy to the people you are visit-ing that will doom your contact to failure. Japanese meetings radiate an atmosphere of laid-back urgency, and you should follow suit.

In compiling your itinerary, you should use your agent in Japan, or whoever your company has routine dealings with. A new man moving into the Japan seat in a company should not attempt to do things differently the first time round. If there is a recognised system for organising Japan itineraries within your company, use it yourself, at least for your first trip. Make changes only on the basis of experi-ence, not theory. The Japanese do not like change for the sake of change. If you have no agent and no recognised system of putting itineraries together, start by talking to the Exports to Japan Unit of the Department of Trade and Industry and JETRO (see p. 145). They will be pleased to help. Make sure that your first visits in Tokyo are to the British Embassy commercial department, the British Chamber of Commerce and the Tokyo branch of your company's bank. They can set the scene for you on arrival.

Ian de Stains of the British Chamber of Commerce makes the point clearly: 'Our aim is to assist British businessmen in general, for example in clarifying their thoughts on a joint venture, or in looking for an agent. But people still come out here not having done sufficient homework. They expect it all to fall into place on a five-day trip.' The members of the British Chamber are very helpful to the new-comer. 'There is a willingness of member companies to be generous to people who will be potential competitors. This is a very healthy attitude, but then foreign companies have a small piece of a very large cake, so why not let others have a bit of it too?'

A very sensible and naturally popular way of making initial visits to Japan is to join an outward mission supported by the DTI. These missions are sponsored by trade associations, Chambers of Commerce or other non-profit-making business organisations and give financial support for the first five visits to Japan made by executives of a company. The support amounts to £740 per trip, a sum which was originally based on 50 per cent of the return economy air fare. The DTI sees this support as paying a contribution to the travel costs of the business executive to Japan, and it should not be used as a way to get a contribution to the cost of an extensive business trip around the Far East. There is a minimum-stay requirement of five working days in Japan to qualify for the mission grant, and the participating traveller must also attend the DTI briefing meeting before the mission sets out. The advantages of joining a mission should be seen not only in terms of saving a bit on the air fare; the added benefit of being with a group of like-minded people, and of being able to learn from their experiences as well as your own, makes the trade mission a very good bet. Trade missions also get solid support from the British Embassy, which ensures that missions find as few doors closed to them as possible.

At this point it is worth mentioning that a similar grant is available for companies participating in exhibitions in Japan. The DTI grant for this is also £740, payable for up to two people who will man the exhibition stand for the entire period of an exhibition. The exhibition grant also involves a subsidy for the cost of the exhibition space and a stand within the British area of the exhibition. As with the mission subsidy, any company is eligible for the grant for the first five times it exhibits in Japan. There are both positive and negative points about exhibiting in Japan, but for any organisation that uses exhibitions routinely to bring its products to the market place, this subsidy is an important benefit. For further information on missions and exhibitions, contact your regional DTI office or the DTI Fairs and Promotions Branch (see Appendix).

To finance your visit, make sure you bring traveller's cheques. The use of international credit and charge cards is increasing (especially Visa and American Express), but cash is still the preferred way of settling bills. Hotels offer exchange rates that are not significantly worse than the bank exchange rates and are much more convenient. Shopping outside your hotel will be far easier with cash than with a credit card.

There is a general feeling that Japan is very expensive. Although it is true to say that the hotels and restaurants in central Tokyo can cost you an emperor's ransom, there are still many parts of the city where food, lodging and the other necessities of life are by no means expensive. As Chris Moss of Virgin Atlantic explains, 'If you can move out of the centre of Tokyo, prices are very reasonable. Everybody says that Japan is expensive. Yes it is, if you are in downtown Tokyo. But outside the centre, it is not that bad.' If you eat exclusively in all the best hotels and restaurants, if you travel everywhere by taxi and if you shop only at the Ginza department stores, you will believe that Tokyo is expensive. But the same would apply to a visitor to London who stayed in a hotel on Park Lane, travelled by taxi and shopped only at Harrods or Fortnum & Mason. The Japanese find London expensive.

Travelling to Japan is much easier than it used to be. Four airlines – Virgin Atlantic, British Airways, Japan Airlines and All Nippon Airways – fly direct and non-stop from Heathrow to Narita. The old days of a two-hour, aimless meander around the transit lounge at Anchorage, staring at the stuffed polar bear, or the rigours of a cup of coffee in Moscow, are long past. The non-stop flight is easy and comfortable, especially now that the Japanese airlines have realised that Westerners require greater leg-room. (I am not sure whether this is because Westerners have longer legs or merely because we tend to fidget and rearrange ourselves in flight more often than our Japanese fellow travellers.) However, it is still a long flight, almost 12 hours, and at the other end there is still the problem of jet lag to cope with.

Chris Moss of Virgin Atlantic again: 'We always recommend that there is a day's acclimatisation when you get to Japan, rather than trying to go straight into business meetings. It is a long trip, and though we all try to make it as comfortable as possible, you've got to give yourself that first day.' There is no certain remedy for jet lag. Japan is nine hours ahead of GMT, so a flight taking off from Heathrow in the early afternoon will arrive in Tokyo around 11 a.m. Japan time, which is 2 or 3 a.m. in Britain. You will not have had a proper night's sleep, and your stomach will be telling you it is a different time altogether. Jet lag is not helped by over-eating or getting stuck into vast quantities of the business class champagne. Drinking no alcohol on the flight certainly helps, although you have to drink something as otherwise you can get dehydrated after 12 hours in the air. Taking sleeping pills works for some people, but not everyone, so you have to find your own way of coping with the time difference. The only sure rule is that you will be affected by the imbalance in your body clock, and that you need to allow yourself some time to overcome that imbalance. If you can make sure you have no business appointments on the day you arrive, and force yourself to stay awake until at least 9 p.m. local time, you will increase your chances of getting a reasonable night's sleep, and of waking up reasonably fresh the next morning for your first appointments.

'Narita airport,' says Chris Moss with gentle understatement, 'is certainly a long way out of town.' For the newly arrived visitor, the first challenge is to get into your hotel without spending all the traveller's cheques your accounts department so generously provided. 'Never ever, ever consider taking a taxi from the airport, because it is so expensive. The only real ways of getting into town are to take the Limousine bus service, or the Narita Express, which is a similar service to the Gatwick Express.' The transit time from Narita to downtown Tokyo is just over one hour on a good day, and considerably more if you happen to arrive at peak rush hour times. You should not expect anybody to meet you at the airport as it would take much too much time out of their working day. Unless you are a very important person indeed, you will be left to fend for yourself at Narita.

The Limousine bus service takes you to the Tokyo City Air Terminal at Hakozaki, which is not quite downtown Tokyo but is a short taxi ride from most hotels. Tickets for the service are available in the arrivals lobby, and the buses go every 10 minutes. Use it. From the Tokyo City Air Terminal, most hotels are within 15 minutes reach by taxi. For hotels in the Shinjuku area, there are services direct from Narita to Shinjuku station, and from there it is a short taxi ride to your hotel. Taxis and subways, as we have already seen, are plentiful in Tokyo, so you should not have a problem in getting to your hotel without too much extra pressure on your health or your wallet.

Business Etiquette

Many books have been written about Japanese etiquette in general and business etiquette in particular. There is not room in this chapter to go into great detail about the rights and wrongs of Japanese business etiquette. There are, however, a few simple rules that are worth noting and following.

Business cards (*meishi*) are the most important business tools in

Japan. It is absolutely essential that you have a large supply of them when you arrive, and that you carry them with you wherever you go. It is also essential that they give the correct information in the correct style, to help your Japanese counterparts understand exactly who you are. In Japan, business cards are all the same size, namely 91 x 55 mm, and you should have your cards for Japan made that size. It is normal for them to be printed in English on one side, and in Japanese on the other. Several companies in Britain will prepare Japanese business cards for your trip (see p. 146), and you should avail yourself of their services. Remember to add the country to your company address: just a county and a postcode will not be enough when, six months later, a Japanese executive is shuffling through his collection and trying to remember who you are. On the Japanese language side, you do not need to have your full address translated. If they want to write to you, they will put your British address on the envelope. Just make sure your fax and telephone numbers are on the Japanese side, together with the international dialling code. Make sure you understand how the Japanese is set out, even if you cannot read it. You do not want to present the card upside-down or back to front if you can help it.

At a business meeting, the very first thing that happens, before you sit down, is that cards are exchanged. This is the fundamental procedure of any Japanese business meeting, and it is a major failure of etiquette not to have a *meishi* ready to present to all the participants. As that may be 8 or 10 people, you never go out at the start of a day's meetings in Japan without a good stock in your pockets. To be entirely polite, you should hand your card over with both hands, bowing slightly as you do so. On receiving a card, you should look at it briefly but with clear interest, taking in what it says about the donor. If there are many new faces, it is quite normal to set out the cards you have just received on the table in front of you, so that you are able to identify throughout the meeting exactly who does what. What you must not do is show any disrespect for the cards now in your possession, because this would be showing disrespect for the company as well as the man you are dealing with. Above all, do not write on them while the meeting is in progress. Once you have got back to your office or hotel, it is quite usual to write perhaps the date and the place of the meeting on the cards, so that you have that as an extra *aide-mémoire*.

'Japanese etiquette is never one-sided. You don't just take, you have to give as well.' Kyoko Harris, a teacher of business Japanese to foreigners, states in simple terms the problem which all visitors dread: the need to give presents to people you do business with. What used to be viewed as the never-ending spiral of gift-giving is no real problem these days. It is normal to bring in a bottle of Scotch or something similar for your agent, but it is not usual to have to give presents to all and sundry as you move from meeting to meeting. The Japanese give business gifts on three occasions: at the two gift seasons of Chugen (June/July) and Seibo (December), and to commemorate a significant business milestone. If you feel your first visit to Japan fits this description, take a few presents to give to the people you do business with. They should be of no great value and have some relevance to your company or your company's country. British executives find that small pieces of Wedgwood pottery are good business gifts, as are any golfing accessories which have genuine Scottish connections. They should be as beautifully wrapped as possible, and you should not be offended if the person you give it to does not open it immediately. It is not the Japanese custom to open presents in the presence of the giver. However, many Japanese are aware of the Western custom, and may therefore open the package there and then. If your visit is not meant to be a significant business milestone, just take a good stock of your company's brochures, annual reports and, if relevant, product samples. These should be given out without stinting to all who require them.

You should never be tempted to use money under the table as a way of making progress in Japan. 'There are amounts of naughty money in Japan,' says Ben Thorne, 'but bribery is political rather than commercial, so I would advise everybody not to get involved. In the commercial sector it is not necessary, so it will not help.' In construction, which is more closely linked to the *yakuza*, the remarkably well-organised gangster groups, than most industries, there may be a problem with the need for financial irregularities, but in almost every other commercial sector bribery is not a factor.

Andrew Lawson of the CBI makes a further point about Japanese business styles. 'The Japanese are honest in their dealings. They are not crooks. They are not the sort of people who let you down or go behind your back. There is a great deal of honour in their dealings. To that extent it is easier to do business in Japan than in some other countries. They will drive a hard bargain, and they will check up on you, but they never do anything underhand.'

The etiquette of Japanese business is not the non-tariff barrier it is sometimes made out to be. There are, of course, bound to be occasions when you do not know what is the correct procedure in a particular circumstance, and there will be occasions when you get it wrong. However, if at those times you at least act in a way that would be polite in your home country, your apologies for any terrible mistakes will be accepted. Left-handedness is, for example, deemed to be impolite. All Japanese are trained to be right-handed, and it is very rare indeed to see a Japanese writing with his or her left hand. There is a colloquial word for left-handed which literally means 'drunk-handed'. The logic behind this is that any Japanese who may be by nature left-handed only reveal this fact when they let their social façade slip after a few drinks. Using chopsticks in the left hand is not the done thing, nor is handing over a business card with the left hand. This creates problems for a left-hander visiting the country, who tends to take the view that eating successfully with chopsticks in the left hand is more polite than spilling everything down his shirt from chopsticks in the right hand. Once more, the Japanese art of compromise, of finding the best solution even if there is no ideal one, comes into play.

Perhaps the worst offence a business visitor is likely to commit is that of being late for a meeting. The Japanese take appointment times to mean the time by which everybody will have arrived for the meeting, so to be even a couple of minutes late is a gaffe. Make sure you leave plenty of time to get from one place to another, and rely on the subways and trains rather than taxis. Getting stuck in a traffic jam in Tokyo is no excuse when you are half an hour late for a meeting you would easily have reached on time if you had taken the subway. Have a cup of coffee in a nearby coffee shop if you are early. You will see many other men in dark blue suits sipping coffee and looking at their watches every couple of minutes. They are also early for their appointments and are waiting until it is polite to arrive at their destination, usually no more than five minutes before the meeting is due to start.

It is very impolite to blow your nose in public in Japan. To do so in a meeting, even one you have arrived on time for, would be seen as the height of bad manners, whereas a succession of sniffs would be acceptable. If you were not aware of this, and were to blow your nose in a meeting with the Japanese, they would quite probably understand that this was the Western way, and with any luck not be particularly offended by your action. If you were to wipe your nose on your sleeve, an action equally disgusting in both Eastern and Western hemispheres, you would be less likely to be forgiven.

A longstanding Tokyo resident tells the story of his vice-chairman, a very large man, who came out from head office on a first visit to Japan, and was taken to meet the chief executive of a major Japanese industrial combine. (Names have been eliminated to protect the guilty and the longstanding Tokyo resident's job). They were shown into the special presidential lift which took them non-stop to the very top floor, where they were met by a young lady in a kimono who ushered them into the chief executive's massive meeting-room. They were invited to sit down on a sofa by a low table, above which hung a beautiful Van Gogh painting of irises which might not have been a copy, and the kimono-clad office lady shuffled out again. A minute later the president and his personal assistant came in. In accordance with correct business procedure, both British businessmen stood up and cards were exchanged. They all sat down and the small talk began. The president spoke only in Japanese, and his personal assistant translated. Although the longstanding Tokyo resident could speak good Japanese, he knew it was right to allow the president's PA to take on the role of interpreter for the meeting.

At this point, the kimono lady came back in bearing Japanese tea, *ocha*, for the assembled company. It had been perfectly prepared in accordance with tea ceremony principles, and the foaming green broth in perfect ceramic bowls was placed in front of each man. The president said '*Itadakimasu*' (a kind of Japanese cross between saying grace and '*bon appétit*'), and three people lifted their tea to their lips. The exception was the British vice-chairman who began fishing inside his pockets for something. After much confusion and disturbance, inevitable when a man the size of a small buffalo wriggles about on a low sofa, the vice-chairman pulled from his jacket pocket a saccharin dispenser. He then quickly popped two tablets into his *ocha*. At this point, the longstanding Tokyo resident's jaw went limp, and he could only hope that the floor would open up immediately and swallow him whole. Before that could happen, however, his vice-chairman began fidgeting again. After another few seconds of frenzied activity, he fished out from a different pocket a swizzle stick from the bar he had been in the night before. He then used this to stir his tea, before licking it and putting it back in his pocket.

Almost every rule of tea-drinking etiquette had been broken in those few seconds, but the only reaction on the Japanese side was for the president to turn to his PA and say, in Japanese of course, 'I have never seen that done before.' Yet despite this terrible beginning to the meeting, as time passed it became clear that the British vice-chairman and the Japanese chief executive had many common interests and opinions, and within six months they had concluded a licence agreement that brought British technology to Japan. The moral of the story is that however bad the breach of etiquette might be, it is still possible to build a business relationship if there is a sincere desire to do so.

The Role of the Trading Companies

The role of the trading companies has for many years been central to the success of the Japanese economy. The routine way of establishing a bridgehead for your products in Japan was to export through a local agent and hope that the business grew. (The term 'agent' is used to describe the role played by a Japan-based company that acts as importer and/or distributor for a British exporter. It does not necessarily mean, of course, that the importer would be legally empowered to act on behalf of the exporter, which is the true commercial definition of the word 'agent'.) Allowing the business to grow at arm's length is not the way either exporters or the trading companies work these days. Nowadays trading houses in Japan are increasingly involved in joint ventures, brokerage and corporate marriages, and the simple export deal is certainly not the only option, and less and less the right long-term plan, for a British company sizing up the Japanese market.

However, as Bob Pearce, who worked for many years with the trading company Cornes & Co., says, 'There has to be a compromise between what one would like to achieve, maybe a fully owned subsidiary company in Japan, and what is economically feasible. Before you look for a joint venture partner, try to find an agent.' The key factor, in Pearce's view, is that the agent should be a specialist in your market sector. 'Look for the specialist, somebody who can immediately understand your product's potential. These days one has to be looking for a niche market.' Gordon Williams, recently Consul-General in Osaka, agrees. 'The market is segmenting, but Japanese production is beginning to cater for niche markets on mass production lines. For example, Toyota can make

10 different models on one production line, all with the same engine.' To try to establish a level playing field, to look for something better than a draw away from home, it is important to have available the specialist skills of an agent who already operates in your market niche, and who can give you the clearest idea of how to make progress in Japan.

The natural corollary to this is the need to spend a great deal of time on early visits on market research. Market research can come from a wide variety of people and places. Paul Brankin of Oxford Instruments believes that the best sources of market information are dealers and customers. 'Our distributors were amazingly open to me. One even said, "We are already manufacturing in opposition to you." And whenever I visited one of the end users, I always found out something I hadn't known before.' Market information can come from official sources, such as the British Embassy, the DTI or JETRO, but it can also be useful to talk to banks, to advertising agencies, to competitors and also, of course, to your agent.

The role of an agent in Japan, in Bob Pearce's view, is to be a true middleman. 'A Japanese company acting as your agent does not want to give you bad news. Winning the confidence of a Japanese agent or customer so that he gives you bad news is 50 per cent of the struggle.' A Japanese will tell you the truth and nothing but the truth, but not necessarily the whole truth. What he misses out are the bits he thinks you do not want to hear, but which are very often the key to your company's potential success in Japan. If he tells you the bad news, this is a service of tremendous importance, and it is something the exporter should appreciate, and not denigrate. 'For an agent to get this message across is terribly important,' says Pearce. 'Sometimes each side of the supplier/customer fence thinks the agent is taking the other side. When you get a broadside from both sides, you know you are doing your job.'

Many major British companies still work through an agent (Cornes handle British Aerospace and Rolls Royce Motors, for example), and this solution can often be the best for the long term as well as the short. Cornes' investment in the Rolls Royce business is described as 'horrendous', involving the setting up of an import, distribution and dealership network in the three major cities, Tokyo, Osaka and Nagoya. Rolls Royce appointed Cornes as their distributor some 40 years ago, but to begin with it was very hard to sell any cars at all. 'The excuse was "I can't buy a Rolls Royce because the emperor has one",' remembers Pearce. 'Our reply was "No – he has two, so there's nothing wrong in you buying one."' All the same, by 1971 only nine Rolls-Royces had been sold in Japan and in 1972 13. By 1978 the total imported had soared to 78, but with the second oil shock the number imported slumped in 1980 to only 20 cars. 'David Plastow, chairman of Rolls-Royce, took the view that in the long term Japan would be an important market, so he was prepared to support our efforts fully. They have put a resident motor-car representative in Japan, and they support us against the activities of the grey-market dealer, the parallel importer.' Under existing laws in Japan it is illegal, as a restraint of trade, to appoint a sole agent. It is legal to support just one company as your importer and as the only organisation authorised to market your goods, but you have no redress against a company that acquires your products legally anywhere in the world for resale in Japan. These parallel imports, by an unauthorised dealer in competition with your appointed agent, have become a serious problem in certain market sectors because the parallel importer does not have to spend any significant money on marketing or holding stocks and can therefore undercut the prices offered by the officially appointed agent. This lowers the market prices unrealistically, in many cases preventing the authorised agent from supporting his marketing activity properly. 'As soon as it gets tough, the grey-market dealer goes to ground,' says Pearce, 'so the support Rolls-Royce gives us pays off for them. By 1991 Japan was the top export market for Rolls-Royce, with 400 cars sold.'

'Rolls-Royce and Bentley motor cars are very expensive in Japan. There is some competition from Mercedes Benz and so on, but the customer has to make a commitment to buy such a thing as a Rolls-Royce. The crux of it is that in Japan, the Silver Spirit four-door saloon is the lowest selling model of all. Japan is the only country that has any realistic sale of the long-wheelbase Bentley Turbo, the most expensive model of all. In the United States they cannot sell that model. But in Japan it is the best seller of all. Its virtues are that it is unostentatious, and the customer has just bought the most powerful, the most brutal, the most beautiful car that he could.'

Rolls-Royce works closely with Cornes, but Paul Brankin of Oxford Instruments has doubts about the wisdom of getting too close to a distributor, especially in their business of industrial instrumentation. 'It can be a satisfactory way of doing some business,' he says, 'but not of maximising it.' Oxford Instruments, however, did not work with just one importer, but set up a network of distributors, each of whom dealt with them on a direct basis. 'Doing business with distributors is not the way to build the future business. The type of distributors one finds fall broadly into two categories. They are either manufacturers themselves of similar sorts of products or they are trading companies. The trading companies' interest is always to maximise their profit, so they are not a vehicle for maximising your market share. Manufacturers, on the other hand, are nearly always filling out their own product line with your products. If the market share grows to anything significant, they will certainly copy it. It is not a case of might, or you've got to worry about it: they absolutely will copy it, because they will see that as essential to the business, to have their own source for that product. So neither option is a way to maximise your business in Japan.'

The Mechanics of Export

There is nothing unusual or complicated about selling goods to Japan, compared with selling goods to other parts of the world. As a general rule, the market is very open, and dealing with the Japanese authorities is normally straightforward. It may well take a little time, but it is straightforward.

Goods for export to Japan have in many cases to be approved by the relevant authorities there, a process which ranges from the wearisome efforts involved in registering medical products for sale, to the virtual lack of any official authorisation needed to import, say, textiles. In each case, you will need to check what approvals are required, but it is fair to say that the Japanese are nowadays fully co-operative members of the international trading community, and for most products it is easier to import into Japan than to almost any other country in the world. The tariff and non-tariff barriers have all but disappeared.

Shipping goods into Japan is straightforward. Vessels sail frequently between Britain and Japan, and between North Europe and Japan. Freight rates are standard. 'There is nothing strange about the insurance of goods, either,' says Tony Dyson of Japan England Insurance Brokers. 'Rates in Japan are unbelievably high, but insurance cover and insurance claims are straightforward.' All the major British insurance companies are established in Tokyo, which is the centre of Japanese insurance. There are also three or four international insurance brokers with offices in Tokyo, although they are not allowed by the Ministry of Finance to act as brokers in Japan. They are therefore registered as 'insurance intermediaries', which, says Dyson, is rather like being an agent. The foreign-owned insurance companies, on the other hand, are registered to act exactly like their Japanese counterparts which still dominate the local insurance market. Foreign-owned insurance companies are not allowed to deal in life policies, but otherwise they work on equal terms. 'The foreign share of the insurance market is peanuts,' says Tim Bridgman of Swire Japan, who act as agent for several non-Japanese insurance companies. 'It is perhaps 2 per cent to 3 per cent, but they all make a lot of profit on it.'

Insurance in Japan is all tariff rated. There are standard premiums for standard risks from fire, earthquake, motor liability, burglary and freight, for example. Every premium has the same wording and the same terms from every insurance company. 'There may be a slight variation for the very big boys,' says Dyson, 'but that's all.' English translations of the standard Japanese terms and conditions are available from every Japanese company which deals in international business. The only word of advice Dyson has for foreign businessmen dealing with insurance companies in Japan is, 'If the Japanese say, "We'll send our man from the Yasuda or wherever round," don't agree to it. Use a foreign broker, even if he is officially just an insurance intermediary. That way everybody will understand what is going on.'

There is no special difficulty with claims, either. 'The Japanese can be very detailed and very thorough,' according to Dyson. 'They ask questions like "Did you leave the hairbrush on this side of the table or the other?". But that's the way they deal with everybody and everything'.

Getting goods through Customs is not difficult. Provided that the goods shipped are the goods listed on the Bill of Lading or the Airwaybill, and provided they are not prohibited for some reason (for example, they are firearms, drugs, or pornographic materials), Customs clearance is simple. Your Customs broker will not be cheap, but that is the way of Japanese business, and you will not be at a disadvantage against your competitors in paying the going rates for your import/warehousing service. All experienced import houses have staff whose entire job is concerned with getting goods safely and efficiently through Customs, so this should not be a problem in your business dealings with Japan. If it is, or if it is given as a reason for your product's failure, do not believe it. Look for the real reason elsewhere.

Jardines Wines and Spirits KK – A Case History

Jardines Wines and Spirits KK is a joint venture established in April 1988 by Jardine Matheson, Moët Hennessy and United Distillers, the spirits arm of Guinness. Each partner has roughly one-third of the equity. The president is Mark Bedingham, an Englishman who has been in Japan for 13 years with Jardine Matheson (one of only three British or part-British companies among the top 50 foreign firms in Japan: the others are Shell and ICI) and who speaks fluent Japanese. Both Louis Vuitton Moët Hennessy and United Distillers have foreign representatives on the board, but the leading role is played by Bedingham. The company distributes many, but not all, of the United Distillers product range, and all of the LVMH wines and spirits product range apart from Veuve Cliquot champagne. 'Our turnover last year was ¥107 billion, and this year will be approximately ¥125 billion, just under one billion US dollars,' says Bedingham. 'We are the biggest importer of wines and spirits, and as of 1990 we are the second largest company measured by revenue of all wines and spirits companies in Japan.'

Importing wines and spirits into Japan was for many years one of the most difficult ways to earn a living. Imports were strictly controlled, with tiny quotas and massive tariffs applying to most spirits, especially Scotch whisky. Nowadays, things have changed, like almost everything in Japan. 'For wines and spirits,' says Bedingham, 'for all effective purposes, the market is completely open. There are some significant improvements that we would still like to see made, that would increase import penetration, but there are indeed no non-tariff or tariff barriers which could effectively restrict your share of the market.'

In 1989, the structure of taxes on wines and spirits was entirely reformed. 'That was I think, a very significant event, although not perhaps in the way it was commonly perceived, which was simply as an opportunity to reduce prices to domestic producers' levels. I never saw it as that. I saw it as an opportunity to reposition certain brands which as tax had changed and as exchange rates had changed had been marooned at inappropriate price points, or which were in the wrong part of the market. You had a chance to reshuffle the pack, knowing that your Japanese competitors would also have to do so at the same time. It also gave an opportunity to generate huge additional funds for advertising and promotion which, in my view, is the most critical element in the wines and spirits business if you are to be successful in Japan. However, the tax reforms were only partial. We have still ended up with tax rate discrimination against whiskies – not, of course, only imported whiskies, but all whiskies. We believe that all those tax rates should be unified.

'We also know that duty rates for products entering Japan are much higher than American or European duty levels. As part of the GATT round, the EC Commission is trying to negotiate reductions in wines and spirits duty rates. Typically, a Scotch whisky would attract around ¥160 to ¥170 a bottle. An equivalent rate going into the States would be ¥10 to ¥15. The European Community rate is higher, but it is still only around ¥30 or ¥40.' That seems to discriminate in favour of whiskies that are manufactured in Japan, and bulk imports are duty free. Kirin, the Japanese beer and spirits giant, for example, brings in whisky in bulk, duty free, which they brand Robert Brown and bottle in Japan. It retails at a much lower price than White Horse, Jardine's market-leading Scotch whisky.

'We also want to see improvements in product definitions,' says Bedingham. 'As we all know, Japan has typically used strict product definitions to limit imports. In our case, we would actually like to see stricter product definitions to improve the quality advantage the European products have. Basically the definitions of what is whisky, what is brandy are vague, allowing domestic producers to use lower cost raw materials than are used for the much higher quality definitions that apply in the States or Europe.'

What are the main factors that have enabled Jardines Wines and Spirits to become so successful? 'Well, I suppose in this business, like so many businesses in Japan, it helps if you started a long time ago. Merely the fact that you have a name which has been well established in the trade gives you a credibility about new initiatives that you seek to implement on a yearly basis. Each new initiative is more favourably received simply because you have been around a long time.

'We have also been innovative in product and packaging introduction, and have done considerable research to introduce packaging and product – the liquid in the bottle – which is well adapted to Japanese taste. White Horse is an example. Internationally there has always been the standard White Horse, but we introduced in 1982 a grade above that, something called White Horse Extra Fine, which was packaged and researched and launched only in the Japanese market. Recently, we have taken that a stage further and launched the single malt which is most associated with White Horse because it is a constituent part of the blend, something called Glenelgin, again exclusively for the Japanese market. This is a blend which we know is very acceptable here. We have now come back to upgrading the standard White Horse sold in the market with packaging and an eight-year-old age statement which again is exclusive to Japan. White Horse is typically an off-premise retail brand in the UK but here in Japan it is a more on-premise higher image brand.'

Updating a product for the Japanese market always means producing a higher quality product than is available elsewhere. This is a feature of the marketing of a massive range of imported products. All the companies whose experience in Japan was drawn on for this book, companies whose products range from luxury motor cars to glass and chinaware, from medical equipment and in-flight services to whisky and scientific instruments, agree that you must be prepared to create a special range of products for the Japanese consumer, and that this range of products will be of higher quality than would satisfy consumers in other parts of the world.

'It is important continually to improve packaging and presentation and to look for new product introduction opportunities,' says Bedingham. 'This is a deceptive market-place. Sometimes it appears to move with glacial speed, and other times it goes through boom-bust cycles which are faster than any European manufacturer can adjust to instantaneously. So you always have to be looking for new opportunities that you are capable of exploiting. By that I mean there is no point in trying to chase the latest fad if the European factory is never going to be able to gear up in time. You have got to have a good understanding of what is going on here but also a pretty good understanding of what is possible in Europe.'

Distribution is a part of the Japanese system which appals foreign companies when they first look at the opportunities in Japan. How does Jardines get through the maze of distribution 'cushions' as they are called? (The cushions seem to work in the snooker sense that to get nearer your goal, you have to bounce off in a number of confusing directions, which only makes the whole process slower, although aesthetically more pleasing than the direct approach.) 'We distribute in the same way that domestic manufacturers distribute, through a layer of primary wholesalers who invoice on to secondary wholesalers, but we frequently negotiate directly with those secondary wholesalers in terms of promotional support. We will also negotiate about promotion at the level of department stores, hotels and a certain number of bars and clubs. We don't find the distribution system, frankly, any kind of barrier to our operation. The credit risk function that the distribution system has is, we think, quite beneficial. We are not anxious to change it.'

This is not because price is an insignificant factor in the buying decision and that the costs of the distribution network can be easily borne. 'Price for all of our products is very much related to the sector of the market. So White Horse goes after less expensive personal entertainment, snack bars and so on; Hennessy goes after the corporate entertaining and clubs. If you go out of the price zone for that target market then you don't have any business. The biggest disturbance to prices comes at the lower end through grey market parallel imports.'

Parallel imports are a thorn in the side of all importers of major international brand products. According to Bedingham, 'There are only two solutions. Either you have excellent control in the rest of the world, so that you can control what is coming into Japan, or you have a marketing strategy which helps you deal with the question of parallel imports. Parallels are very pernicious because even if the quantities were to reduce on a year by year basis, their real effect is still that they tend to set pricing in the trade. Your products are continually compared against the price of parallels, which may lead to a loss of trade confidence and always leads to a loss of trade profitability. So, obviously, if you are introducing brands which are exclusive to the market, they cannot be paralleled.'

The Japanese government originally encouraged the practice of parallel importing, as we have seen, when they banned the appointment of sole agency and distribution agreements. They did this in the hope that there would be an end to price fixing and unreasonable profits by sole importers, but this is not what has happened. 'We are not optimistic,' says Bedingham, 'about persuading the Japanese government that parallels are not achieving the objectives the government had set itself. They have not proved a successful policy in improving the quantity or the quality of imports into Japan. It will be some time before the Japanese government take it seriously, but we say that investment is more difficult in a market where parallels are an influence.'

An Open Market

'The position of the British government,' I was told, 'is that the Japanese market is open.' Many would be surprised that any British government could take up a position so close to the truth, but the reality is that to all intents and purposes, the Japanese market, at least administratively and legally, is open. The arguments of price and legislation no longer apply. 'Providing the price is acceptable,' says Hiroshi Mikami of Japan Medico, a company which imports tens of billions of yen worth of medical goods each year, 'all we really worry about is quality and delivery.' All sorts of products from all over the world are readily available to the Japanese consumer and to Japanese industry, but the one area where Japan is still not fully open is in the minds of the Japanese themselves. No legislation will persuade a Japanese to choose a foreign product over a home-made one, even if legislation can ensure that he or she is given the choice. In Virgin's Megastore in Shinjuku, compact discs imported from the United States cost ¥2100. A domestically produced version of the same CD, sounding identical in every way, will cost ¥2500 or so, but still there is a strong market for the Japanese version. If you move down the road to a Japanese record store, there will be a much greater stock of the local product than there is at Virgin's Megastore, there will be much larger crowds inspecting the racks, and the percentage of higher priced product actually bought will be significantly greater.

Japan as an export market is now open, but it requires a great deal of time and care to keep it open for your products. Finding an import agent and a reliable distribution network are the first priorities for the exporter setting up business in Japan. However, for many products, the long-term interests of both exporter and customer are better served by the establishment of a more permanent base in Japan.

CHAPTER 6

SUBSIDIARIES AND JOINT VENTURES

'Frankly, if you are really serious about doing business in Japan,' says Ian de Stains of the British Chamber of Commerce in Tokyo, 'you have got to be here. The days of visits every six months are over.'

The establishment of a more permanent base in Japan can take a number of different forms. As a first step, a company can place a member of its staff permanently in Japan, inside the office of its agent or distributor, to help the agent in its work. Getting a little deeper into the Japanese market, it can establish a representative office, to oversee its activities in Japan on a more independent basis, but without trading in its own right. It can license its technology or products to a Japanese company for a lump sum or a royalty, or a combination of the two. It can establish its own branch office in Japan or, taking it one stage further, its own subsidiary Japanese company. It can also consider a joint venture with a Japanese company to manufacture or market its products in Japan. These are the options which would be available to any company looking at any new market, and all these options are possible within Japan.

There are no generalisations about the 'right way' to go deeper into the Japanese market: each company must look at its own situation. Having said that, the options of a fully owned subsidiary and a local joint venture are the most commonly used methods.

Establishing a representative office is a straightforward matter. Unless your parent company is a bank or insurance or securities firm, in which case Ministry of Finance regulations apply, a foreign-owned representative office does not have to be registered with the Legal Affairs Bureau. There are no official approvals required, provided that the representative office does not take part in any direct profit-making activity. It may get involved in advertising and market research, and it can act as adviser and consultant to other companies on its parent company's business in Japan. As long as a representative company does not engage in any commercial activity, for tax purposes it is not deemed to be a permanent business establishment, and is therefore not subject to taxation. There is a certain degree of flexibility

in defining the types of 'commercial activity' it may participate in,
but if, for example, you want your local representative to spend
much of his time negotiating deals on behalf of the parent, or secur-
ing business in a manner that would imply he was acting as a local
agent, then the tax office may take a different view. It may decide
that the representative office is actually an agent and therefore
liable to corporation tax on the profits deemed to have been gen-
erated by the office's business activities, whether or not those profits
are actually made in Japan.

Funds to establish and maintain the representative office can be
freely remitted to Japan without any problem. The costs are not
totally unreasonable. It will cost between ¥750,000 and ¥1 million
a month for an apartment for your representative to live in and, as
a salary, a figure around double what he is earning in the UK. The
high end of the salary scale is therefore likely to be about ¥25
million a year. The total cost of keeping a married man with no
school-age children in Tokyo, with office expenses as well, will run
to about ¥50 million a year, say £315 000.

British Telecom's history in Japan is typical of the way a company has moved closer to the heart of Japanese industry by a logical
progression of deepening relationships. 'There is nothing clever or
exceptional about what we have done,' says George Newns of BT.
'Six years ago, we established a representative office with one man
and a secretary. It grew. By 1988 the business had grown sufficiently for us to decide to form our own KK.'

A KK is a *kabushiki kaisha* or limited company. The establishment
of a KK is not difficult; it merely takes time. The incorporation of a
joint-stock company in Japan has to comply with the Commercial
Law, as do the auditing, accounting and working procedures of the
company, but none of these procedures is sufficiently removed from
Western practice to cause difficulties. Step one is to find a good
commercial lawyer because without legal advice you will not be
able to set up the company successfully. It is said that for every 10
engineers in Japan, there is only one qualified lawyer, while in
America there are 10 lawyers for every qualified engineer. Japan is
not a litigious country, and the law is used to settle differences only
as a last resort, but in establishing a company, or making significant
changes to the way your business is structured in Japan, you must
have legal advice.

'It is extremely important to have very good local professional advice,' says Malcolm Carlisle of Smiths Industries Medical Systems. 'Japan, because of its recent history, has got a legal system which is based on Anglo-Saxon principles. It's the code of law which the American put in there after the war, so the basics of the law are not very different from what we would understand in the UK or America. That is helpful in that you can start out structuring these arrangements in the way you would an English or American transaction, and you can get a long way on the business parameters before you need local professional advice. But at a certain point you need your Japanese lawyer with you.'

In forming a *kabushiki kaisha* there must be seven or more sponsors, who must be resident in Japan. These people usually come from the legal or accounting office you appoint to help in the creation of the KK, and the common practice is for each sponsor to buy one share and for the foreign investor to buy the rest of the shares. Once the company is established, the foreign investor buys the remaining seven shares from the sponsors and is thus the proud possessor of a fully owned subsidiary company in Japan. This is not as simple as it seems because under the Foreign Exchange Law a foreign investor must give the Ministry of Finance three months' notice of his intention to buy the shares. It will certainly take you longer than you expect to get your subsidiary up and running, but, provided that you have patience and persistence, a sensible time scale and good legal advice, it is not a complicated process.

'The minimum paid-up capitalisation for a KK must be at least 25 per cent of the authorised capital,' says Ian de Stains of the British Chamber of Commerce, so for a ¥20 million company, you would have to pay in ¥5 million at least, say £32,000. But this is not usually a factor in deciding whether to set up a company. 'If you need to ask the price, you cannot afford it.' But the rules have changed, and will probably keep changing, generally in a liberalising direction. The administrative barriers to setting up a subsidiary in Japan are getting lower all the time.

Oxford Instruments – a Case History

'The business of the Oxford Instruments Group is advanced instrumentation. Established some 35 years ago, its products are used today for scientific research, chemical analysis and quality control, patient monitoring, semiconductor processing and diagnostic imaging. Eighty-five per cent of its sales are to markets outside the UK.

Oxford Instruments is recognised as a world leader in several technologies, particularly in those relating to superconducting magnets.' The 1994 Report and Accounts of Oxford Instruments also showed the Witney-based group had an annual turnover of over £110 million.

Dr Paul Brankin is now Director of Operations, Japan for Oxford Instruments. 'In October 1989 we established a tiny representative office in Japan, with one man and a secretary, just 300 square feet.' The question was where to go from there. 'Our chairman, Peter Williams, realised that while we, as a high-technology company, were very satisfied with the level of our business in Japan – a few millions – yet when you looked at the growth in Japan during the late 1980s when the yen was revalued against the dollar, we were actually underperforming relative to other markets. In other words, we were doing less business in Japan than we were in Germany, and a very great deal less than in the United States.' The actual figures for 1990, as published in the Report and Accounts, show that turnover in America was almost £35 million, in Germany £12 million but in Japan only £7.5 million. 'So Peter Williams called together a meeting in April 1990 of the heads of the various operating divisions and people responsible for Japan, and I came along. The view of the meeting was that we were pretty content with what we were doing in Japan. We recognised what the chairman said, that it should be a lot better, but we did not see any easy way of making it a lot better, and we know a lot of people doing worse. We could spend money trying to make it better, so while we generally support the idea of looking at it, we are not really clear where we should go. That was the rationale for me going out to Japan for a long period of time. We did not have much clear data, and when you have 10 to 12 distributors, it is even hard to do a clear analysis of what you are doing through all the distributors.'

Brankin went out to Japan in September 1990. 'I was available, interested and it was a job that needed doing. And I suppose the one qualification that I had was that I knew more about the spectrum of the group's businesses than anybody else. I had a pretty broad knowledge of the group and a number of the people in it, which was very helpful because a key task was spending a lot of time talking to all the people and achieving a consensus, to use a Japanese way of thinking.' A long career within one company, leading to a senior rank, and a willingness to listen, are two attributes which the Japanese appreciate. Brankin was very well qualified to represent the interests of Oxford Instruments in Japan.

His first trip lasted six weeks. 'I produced a report which was very factual. The conclusion was that we were not doing well in Japan both in a quantitative and a qualitative sense. Our name was virtually unknown there, our distribution organisation had serious weaknesses and we hadn't any sort of a base for doing any better. Within our 1500 employees we only had two Japanese speakers, and only about 20 people who had any experience of Japan. I learnt as a very sharp lesson that if we compared ourselves with a Japanese company of maybe a slightly larger size, out of say 3000 employees they would have a few hundred English speakers and one or two hundred people who had spent a significant time in the West, either in America or Europe. So we really were not playing on a level playing field. We had only two Japanese speakers, and although we had two people who had been on more than 50 trips to Japan, all the visits had been for less than three weeks.' Brankin believes that business trips are not enough to get to grips with the business culture of Japan. 'Even if you have been to Japan a hundred times, if each visit is for only two weeks the experience of actually working there for a few months is quite different.'

'We had no organisation except the vital base of a representative office, a little room where we could set up some meetings, and a telephone number to put on the *meishi*. It was not desperately expensive, but my report said that we had no real infrastructure, and the only option available to us if we wanted to grow our business was to set up our own company.'

There are many sources of advice when a foreign company decides to move into Japan. Brankin spoke to most of them. Perhaps surprisingly, he felt that Japanese banks gave him more insight into his direct business problems than some of the more obvious organisations like the British Embassy or JETRO. The British Chamber of Commerce was extremely helpful on logistics, but the banks pin-pointed the particular problem he spent more time on than any other. 'I remember very clearly, when we talked to one of the banks about what the risks were, they said that the biggest problem they had observed among foreign companies setting up in Japan has essentially been a problem with people. There have really been no others.

'It is a bit of a glib generalisation, but they specifically said that it is not very difficult to recruit some people, but that in the long term, doing so is worse than not recruiting any people, because you have them as a millstone and a cost almost for ever, in a Japanese context. Recruiting the wrong people is just as unsatisfactory as not recruiting anybody at all.'

Mike Barrett of the executive research consultancy, GKR Japan, would agree. 'Many foreign companies here, at the beginning, whether or not they were in a joint venture, would certainly have had some help from perhaps a Japanese partner or a Japanese friendly organisation in finding staff. They would have taken on some Japanese second career people, some retirees or people in their 50s. If the companies had got themselves properly established first, by bringing in people at the top they could build from the top down and bring in younger managers. Now they realise that the only way to build for the future is to recruit at graduate level, straight from the universities. That's really become the key for foreign companies in Japan. Everybody is trying to recruit at university level. It's a big struggle. You are in competition with all the big Japanese corporations. So how on earth do you persuade somebody to join XYZ company when XYZ may think it has got a tremendous international reputation, but nobody has ever heard of it here?'

This is the key question for British companies setting up in Japan, and there is no straightforward answer. 'A corporate image will help. If the company is in a consumer goods area it may well have a brand image, which can help it to get across to potential employees. If you are selling Louis Vuitton or Cutty Sark or something, at least people have seen it around and are aware of the brand image. If you are quoted on the Japanese stock exchange, it helps to create business confidence. If you are not quoted, at least it helps to be a *kabushiki kaisha*. In the financial world, people understand that you are probably only a branch for financial and regulatory reasons. But if you are an industrial company, and you have only got a branch or representative office, it is very difficult to get somebody of any seniority or weight to join you, because how long are you going to be there? What is the commitment of the parent company to Japan?'

Oxford Instruments have used headhunters to help them find their president. Other companies have used less subtle methods of recruiting their key coalface workers: by poaching them from the distributors or associate companies their new KK will disenfranchise. That is not as easy in Japan as it might be in other countries, as the tug of company loyalty and long-term job security are difficult to overcome, but if you can recruit without acrimony somebody who already has experience with your products and your customers, and who has a good track record that your company can already vouch for, this will certainly help any newcomer get off to a solid start.

In Paul Brankin's view, there were several key things to do in setting up the company, 'First we had to recruit a president, because he would be the key to recruiting further staff, and until we'd got a president in whom we were confident, we could not really say we were up and running. Secondly, we had actually to register the company, which at first sight was a trivial thing to do but turned out to be not quite so trivial. It was a straightforward, relatively undemanding process, but it did take three months.'

Then there was the problem of finding appropriate premises. Oxford Instruments first went to new offices in Hatchobori. In Tokyo in 1991 it was easy to find reasonably priced property, and things have not changed dramatically since. The office was in a brand-new building, and they occupied a whole floor, around 1000 square feet at round about £25 a square foot. 'Tokyo is well set up for the small start-up type of office,' says Brankin. It may be more difficult and more expensive to find property in central positions like Marunouchi or Shinjuku, but Hatchobori is only three stops on the subway from Ginza, and the price is reasonable. The British Chamber of Commerce has quoted a figure of about £80 per square foot annual rent for a prestigious area of Tokyo, with the requirement, often, for 24 months' rental in advance. As the standard office rental agreement is for 24 months, this means you pay your entire rent up front, at least for the period of the first contract.

'The next thing to do is to set up a relationship with a bank, particularly borrowing facilities. That was relatively easy to do. We talked to two or three banks and found that we got on particularly well with one of them, so settled on it. It is a Japanese bank with an office in London, and it has been very helpful indeed. It acted as the depository for the subscription to the company in forming the KK so it has had an important role to play. It is on one level a trivial matter, but it is also a vitally important matter in terms of the relationship. Given the small size of our operation, it has been exceedingly helpful. The lending rates we have been offered are exceptionally good compared with lending rates for similar sums in the UK. And accounting was easy. Peat Marwick are our auditors around the world, so it was not an issue.'

The final problem was in telling all the distributors what was happening, a problem compounded by having to manage the process of establishing a company while keeping 12 distributors in the dark. 'We felt it was really important it was managed properly,' says Brankin. 'What we did was get the company legally established, which happened on 27 June 1991, and then we set up a reception at the Hotel Okura on 26 July. After we had sent out the invitations to this reception (and there was nothing unusual about our distributors being invited to a reception because we had had one about a year earlier), we went round to each distributor to see the people we were dealing with on a day-to-day basis, and said, "Just before the reception, our chairman is coming out and we would like to set up a meeting with your chairman. We would like to tell you now what the agenda for that meeting is so that your chairman can be prepared. The one agenda item is, we have established our own company." We thought it through carefully and took advice and it worked beautifully. All we were telling them initially was that there was going to be a meeting, and there was an agenda item, and what that agenda item was.

'When our chairman came, he went into each meeting and said, "We are here to announce the setting up of the company and you are very welcome to the announcement party." He had been pre-warned, and we had already had many conversations about the issues that arose. Generally speaking, there weren't any issues – but, my word, we had had conversations in the meantime. It all went very smoothly, so there were no horrified reactions. The whole shape of the process was important, starting off at a low level so that it was not a big deal, no registered letter arriving on the chairman's desk, saying "You're fired" or anything like that. It was a discussion, really, not the announcement of a decision. The chairmen were able to meet and there was a reception to which all the distributors came. They saw that everybody was being treated in exactly the same way and that they weren't being fed some sort of line. I like to think that was the key in doing that business. A lot of effort went into it, about a month's work in total. It was very important within our own organisation, too, because our biggest concern with the establishment of our own subsidiary had been that the current distributors would think that was the end of the road for them, whether it was or not, and would react violently and immediately turn off. None of that has happened. But internally we had to be sure we did it properly.'

By 1994 the wisdom of setting up in Japan had been proved. Oxford Instruments now employs 30 people in Japan, including three expatriates. They have their head office in Tokyo, sales offices in Tsukuba and Osaka and a Technology Centre at Wakaba in Saitama Prefecture, north of Tokyo. Business in Japan has roughly doubled, and more than 50 per cent of the whole group's growth in 1993/94 came from Japan, which for the first time overtook Germany as the group's second largest overseas market after the USA. 'Where we are today is very close to where we wanted to be, and the path we have taken is pretty much the one we planned in 1991,' says Paul Brankin. 'I don't see that we've made any mistakes, but in an ideal world we would have been even more Japanese about it and taken even more time and trouble over personal and business relationships. But we are still on good terms with all our distributors.'

Oxford Instruments have also tried not to lose sight of the wood for the trees. 'We all of us see that being successful in Japan proves the quality of our products worldwide.'

Joint Ventures

If the establishment of a subsidiary is not seen as the best way forward in Japan, the other most closely studied option is the joint venture. A joint venture is a company limited under Japanese law, most usually a *kabushiki kaisha*, where more than 10 per cent is owned by a foreign partner. Forming a joint venture, from a legal, financial and administrative point of view, is very similar to forming a wholly owned subsidiary. The only significant difference is that the anti-monopoly laws of Japan require that any joint-venture agreement between a foreign investor and a Japanese company or private investor must be filed with the Fair Trade Commission (FTC) within three months of signature of the agreement, and the FTC has the right to withhold approval if it feels that fair competition is hampered by the agreement. The FTC has very broad-ranging theoretical powers and has been known, for example, to force a change in licence royalty rates, but it is very unusual for it to intervene in a joint-venture agreement unless there has been a clear indication from the outset that problems might arise.

The difficulties in a joint venture are always in the relationship between the two partners. It is unusual for a successful joint-venture company to be owned equally by both partners. There is usually a dominant shareholder in any successful JV, even if it is only 51 per cent/49 per cent. The need for one partner to be seen to be the leader is important, although if that is the Western partner, and he uses his majority shareholding to lead in an unnecessarily aggressive way, the JV is going to be in trouble from the beginning.

The possibility of buying into existing Japanese companies is becoming more talked about. The idea of a contested take-over of a Japanese firm by a Western one is still unthinkable, but a friendly investment or even a take-over is becoming an increasingly common means of market entry. The example of British Oxygen's friendly take-over of Osaka Sanso is often cited. On the other hand, the American corporate raider T. Boone Pickens' attempt to take over Koito, a motor parts manufacturer, failed dismally. He managed to acquire a 20 per cent shareholding, but this did not even give him the right to attend shareholders' meetings, let alone have a place on the board. 'I would not say that take-over will be a normal way of entering the Japanese market,' says Paul Dimond, Commercial Counsellor at the British Embassy, 'but it will be increasingly used. If a company wants to be taken over, then the Japanese government would not object. It would take no position unless it were in a strategic area, such as petrochemicals or defence.'

Japan Medico KK – A Case History

Japan Medico KK is a Nagoya-based importer of medical devices, which for over 20 years has distributed Portex single-use medical devices and other Smiths Industries medical products. An announcement by SI on 25 July 1991 stated that, 'Smiths Industries has completed an agreement to acquire 24.5 per cent of the equity of Japan Medico Co. Ltd, at a cost of £3.2 million. Japan Medico will now appoint two directors to its board nominated by Smiths Industries. The other partners are Mr Hiroshi Mikami, founder and president of the company, and the Kuraray Co. Ltd, a leading Japanese chemical manufacturer.' For the record, Kuraray own 51 per cent of the company, and Mr Mikami 24.5 per cent. The joint venture had taken a very long time to reach its final shape, and evolved from a tangled web of relationships and increasing business successes over a quarter of a century.

In 1969, Mikami's company at the time, Japan Anaesthetic Apparatus Company, became importer and distributor of the Portex range of anaesthetic tubing. Portex are a subsidiary of Smiths Industries and make a range of single-use PVC tubes, which, for example, anaesthetists use to control lung function in operating theatres and intensive care units. Up till then, Portex had used Mitsui & Co., a *keiretsu* trading house, whose purchases from Portex in the final year of their distribution agreement amounted to just £150. Mikami's research showed that the existing distribution network could not be made to introduce new medical products successfully, so he set about creating his own network. 'Mr Mikami has a quite remarkable insight into the medical devices business in Japan,' says Malcolm Carlisle of Smiths Industries Medical Systems, acknowledging the first point that any joint venture must reach before success is possible: you must find a good partner. Mikami then created Japan Medico, which, to begin with, was his fully owned private company.

The Portex business began to develop in Japan until there came a time in the early 1970s when Japan Medico needed extra funds if it was to grow the business in the way that Mr Mikami foresaw that it could. There were some discussions between Smiths Industries and Mikami about the possibility of direct investment in Japan Medico at that time, but the talks never reached fruition. At around the same time, Smiths Industries were in discussion with Kuraray on other medical-related matters, and an introduction was made between Japan Medico and Kuraray. In 1976, this finally resulted in Kuraray taking a majority stake in Japan Medico and giving it the capital it needed to grow. At the same time, a new joint venture between Kuraray and Smiths Industries was negotiated. This was called Kuraray-Portex KK, and was designed to be a manufacturing and distribution vehicle for Portex products in Japan, once turnover reached the right levels to justify local manufacture.

However, according to Malcolm Carlisle, 'What actually happened was that Smiths Industries continued to use Japan Medico as its distributor, and the success of that distribution agreement in essence made the joint venture irrelevant. The joint venture was never truly activated. It existed on paper but it didn't ever trade. It never received the distribution rights or manufacturing rights. It was just a shell operation. It could have been a perfectly sensible scheme but it didn't work, not because it was irrational or unviable or silly, but because something better overtook it and left it on the shelf. The Kuraray joint venture became fairly early on a dead letter. The reason why Kuraray did not really care about developing the joint venture was that they owned 75 per cent of Japan Medico, so they could take the attitude that, by being financial masters of the distributor, they got their reward. If Portex and Japan Medico do well together, why disturb it? It isn't broken, so don't let's try and fix it.

'That continued for a good number of years until eventually we started saying to ourselves, "This is getting too big and too successful just to be a distribution arrangement. We have got to a size where we cannot go on and on without some direct involvement".' By this stage, Portex exports to Japan had topped the £10 million mark, and Mikami reckoned he was buying almost 30 per cent of the company's turnover. 'The reason for the recent investment in Japan Medico,' states Carlisle, 'was simply to take the development of this business one step further so that we have very direct interest in the management and operation of the distribution vehicle and are not simply looking at it as a supplier to a customer. We are now also directly involved in the local distribution of our products. What we see coming out of that is a much stronger input into the marketing and sales techniques. Mikami's great business strength is his knowledge and understanding of the distribution system in Japan. What we can lay on top of that is product knowledge, marketing perspectives and the ability to develop further the sales of the products that we have got and introduce alongside them. I'm not saying that Mikami does not have a lot of that ability already himself: he has a very strong team. But having the Portex and SIMS team involved can only help.'

The Smiths Industries involvement is at the highest level. The Chairman of the Medical Systems Group, George Kennedy, is one of the two SI directors on the board of Japan Medico, and he has taken a close personal interest in the development of SIMS business in Japan. Commitment from the top is vital for a company hoping to achieve long-term success in Japan.

The nub of the negotiations to create the joint venture was in persuading Kuraray to give up 24 per cent of their shareholding in Japan Medico, and sell it to Smiths Industries. How did SI persuade them to sell? 'The fundamental argument is that each side benefits from the association with the other. They understood the logic of our position, which was that you don't go on indefinitely building up a business without any direct involvement. There comes a point in any business where you want to be directly involved in your own future. It's too big for you not to be. If something were to go wrong, which I don't for a minute believe will happen, nobody could turn round and say, "Why haven't you got involved and done something about it?" They saw that it was inevitable we got involved. We said that in order to continue with our relationship with Japan Medico, we would need to have some direct involvement. They wanted to maintain the relationship with Portex, which had been a very profitable one, and it was then a question of negotiating what the terms of that acquisition would be.'

The negotiations with Kuraray were wide-ranging. 'It is clearly understood that no party is going to override the other parties' interests just because they have got a majority. Those are things that you cannot legislate for. You can write all sorts of things into an agreement, but fundamentally you have got to have a business understanding. Kuraray's interest is in developing the Portex business because it fuels the profits of Japan Medico. Our interest is exactly the same. That is the reason why it has worked in the past, and why it is going to work in the future.'

By 1994 the proof of the strategy was visible in the results. Japan Medico's turnover had risen to ¥8 700 million (about £54 million), of which 70 per cent was in Smiths Industries' products. SI were not only expanding the sales of their products made in the UK, Europe and the United States; they were also participating in the profits of selling them in Japan. 'The difficulties of getting into the Japanese market were always exaggerated,' says Carlisle. 'The straightforward difficulties of product registration and the like are onerous, but that is not the real problem. The real problem is the distribution system and the need to have a very big investment in the knowledge of how to operate that system.'

The process of serious negotiation over the Smiths Industries investment in Japan Medico took two years. 'With hindsight you can always do things more quickly, but the reason for doing it at that speed was mainly because the objective was to maintain relationships and not to alarm people. I don't think one can overestimate the amount of time that a Japanese corporation likes to take to be comfortable with change. Japan has got a lot of strengths, but they do not operate by individual decision makers. Consequently you are dealing with a team of people which has a spokesman, but which needs to come to a common view, and that takes time. A meeting establishes certain issues, and then they will go away and take a position on it, and then you negotiate from there further.'

'Japan is a long way away. You have to go there to do these

deals. You can't do them by telephone or correspondence, and you can't do them in the UK. People have to be clear on that point. All the papers and all the people are in Japan, and you have to go to them, rather than expect them to come to you.

'One piece of advice I would give is: use a Japanese lawyer, and not a lawyer working for the Japanese branch of an English or American law firm. Our Japanese lawyer was one of the best mergers and acquisitions lawyers I have come across. He was concise, economical and effective, and very useful in the detailed negotiation at the end, which you need to do in Japanese.'

Commercial Law Practice

The law is one area of Japanese commercial life where the doors are still almost shut to foreigners. The Foreign Attorneys Law became effective from 1 April 1987, but this still does not give foreign lawyers any real scope to practise as they would almost anywhere else in the world. Linklaters & Paines, one of Britain's largest commercial law practices, has an office in Tokyo, but, like all foreign law firms, it is not allowed to employ Japanese lawyers nor to give opinions on matters of Japanese law. It does have on its staff one of the nine Japanese nationals who is qualified in English law, but even he is not allowed to practise in Japan. The foreign law firms are in Tokyo not for the business the local market can provide, but to offer a complete global service to their international clients. According to the Foreign Attorneys Law, they are there 'to provide legal services related to the laws of their jurisdiction of qualification.'

The restrictions on foreign legal operations in Japan are not reciprocal. A Japanese law firm in Britain could employ a British qualified lawyer, and its Japanese staff would not have to go through the complicated registration processes that apply to foreign lawyers in Japan. Foreign law firms can only be run by 'registered foreign lawyers' (*gaikokuho jimu bengoshi* or *gaiben*) who have to be registered with the Japan Federation of Bar Associations. One of the qualifications to become a registered foreign lawyer is that you must have been qualified as a lawyer for at least five years under your home jurisdiction. This means that there is no point in sending junior lawyers out to Tokyo for experience. Many Japanese companies will not even discuss matters of foreign law unless a *gaiben* is present.

However, for Linklaters & Paines, there have been unexpected advantages in being in Tokyo. 'Only since setting up a Japanese office and understanding the way that Japanese companies work have we realised the need to get to know people, to establish relationships,' says James Gordon, a solicitor (but not a *gaiben*) based in Tokyo. 'Now in London, in order to get Japanese accounts, we have changed our style, and it works.'

'The playing field is not level in Japan,' says Tony Grundy, one of the two registered foreign lawyers at Linklaters & Paines in Tokyo, 'but that comes from the Japanese way of dealing with the law. Japanese corporations do not have experience in instructing outside lawyers. Within Japanese corporations, as a general rule, the legal departments are staffed by people who are not qualified lawyers, but who have many years experience of the sorts of legal problems a company like theirs has. For example, they might have a lot of intellectual property specialists, people who specialise in patents and licences, and a lot of knowledge of trade issues. In some of the general trading companies, the legal department consists of people who are on a two-year assignment between, say, oil trading and credit assessment. In contrast to the West, where in-house counsel are generalists and out-house counsel are specialists, in Japan there is much greater specialist knowledge in the in-house departments. They would know much more about the law that they regularly deal with than any outside lawyers. They are very knowledgeable and very good at explaining all the relevant facts.'

Great efforts are being made, especially by the United States government, to open the Japanese market fully to foreign lawyers. 'Of the issues on the table at the moment,' says Grundy, 'the most important ones for us are that we would like to practise as a branch in all respects, and to get rid of the confusion that arises because we are all licensed individually. There are other issues like being able to represent foreign parties in arbitration proceedings in Japan, but the crucial issue, so far as the Americans are concerned, is the right to hire Japanese lawyers and to form partnerships with them.' This is the most difficult point, given the shortage of qualified lawyers in Japan. 'There are 500 new qualifiers each year, 200 of whom go to the Public Prosecutor's office, so you have 300 new recruits each year coming to the Japanese bar. To put that into perspective, in Britain Linklaters alone hires 100 recruits each year.' The demand for Japanese lawyers from foreign firms could deprive the domestic system of their entire new intake for years to come. 'Whereas the domestic businesses get on very well without recourse to Japanese lawyers for most of their business, foreign companies coming here need legal advice, and, certainly at the moment, they do not feel they have sufficient access to that advice because there aren't enough lawyers. If Japan wants to grow as an international business centre, the only answer is for the Japanese to train more lawyers.

'What the British company doing business in Japan needs is access to Japanese legal advice. They must recognise the limited knowledge that most Japanese lawyers will have about a lot of the practical problems they are likely to ask about. The Japanese lawyers don't get involved in a range of legal-related matters because it is all done by in-house people or just by direct discussions with administrators without involving lawyers. Of course, it is very difficult if you want to use a lawyer to represent you before one of the Japanese ministries. The approach of those ministries will be that they only deal with principals. What the British company needs is to employ an experi-enced office manager or senior Japanese man who has worked for a Japanese company for 20 years in a field similar to theirs, and who has come across the regulatory problems before and can tell them what the precise position is from a practical point of view.

'The law in Japan is kept vague,' says Grundy. 'The way progress is made is not by changing the law, but by reinterpretation of the provisions. The vaguer and broader they are, the easier it is to do that. The problem with trying to seek that advice from an outside legal adviser is that he won't have the practical experience. The message is: Yes, you definitely need a Japanese lawyer, and you should refer everything where there is any doubt to that lawyer. But recognise that the advice you get may not be the most practical and may be over-cautious, simply because the lawyer does not have the practical experience which someone who has operated in the field will have.'

Multiple Joint Ventures – The Virgin Group

By the end of 1991, the Virgin Group of companies was beginning to look more and more like a Japanese *keiretsu*. There is no overall Virgin holding company, just four separate but horizontally inte-grated companies which between them have vertical links to about 120 operating companies. Japanese partners play an important role in the group structure.

'We now have more links with Japanese companies than with any other nation,' says Will Whitehorn, Director of Corporate Public Relations for Virgin. 'We like the way they like to work, in the long term. To do business in Japan, you should not worry at all about next year or the year after.' Virgin's Japanese partners now include Fujisankei Communications, who own 25 per cent of one of the four holding companies, Virgin Music Group; Marui, who own 50 per cent of Virgin Megastores Japan Ltd; and Seibu Saison, who own 10 per cent of Voyager Travel Holdings, which runs the airline and holiday operations. Virgin also has close working arrangements with companies like video game manufacturer Sega and health drinks manufacturer Otsuka Seiyaku, and there will probably be more Japanese partners over the next few years.

'The way Richard Branson saw the company developing was very easy for the Japanese to understand and accept,' says Whitehorn. 'We are now extremely well known in Japan, so that Japanese companies have confidence that if they do business with us it will work. This puts a huge onus on us to make it work.' He believes that moving quickly is the key, but without putting too much pressure on the Japanese partner. 'There has to be give and take. We have been very stubborn about the way we wanted to do our joint venture deals. So are they. But if you keep talking and keep talking, in the end a deal emerges. You have to take the long-term view.'

For Virgin, Japan is not just a market. It is an international opportunity. 'It is not a question of what we are going to do in Japan, but of what we are going to do with Japanese people, Japanese companies and Japanese finance all around the world.'

CHAPTER 7

MARKETING, SALES PROMOTION AND PUBLIC RELATIONS

The Customer is King

'*Kyakusama wa osama*' – 'the customer is king'. This is the maxim that is repeated constantly in Japan to sum up the Japanese way of marketing. If the customer wants it, he shall have it. All foreign businessmen coming to the country will hear the words within a day or two, sometimes as a proud statement of the way things are, and sometimes as a way of saying 'no' to an over-eager salesman without actually using the n-word.

Like all generalities, it is not entirely true. I remember trying to buy a glass coffee jug in Tokyo to replace the one that our cat had knocked off the table, to be told that the jug could only be bought as part of a set with the electric base, which, despite its best efforts, the cat had not broken. It was impossible to persuade the department store that all this particular customer wanted was the glass jug: I had to buy the whole set or nothing at all. The customer was not king in that particular case. Nor is he when a Japanese gets involved with officialdom, whether it is the local policeman or a junior clerk at the Ministry of Finance or the local City Office. It is the official who acts as though he were king.

Yet almost everywhere in Japanese life you come across standards of service which would be considered remarkable in the West. If you take your car to fill up with petrol, you will be greeted by three or four attendants in uniforms and Wellington boots who not only fill your tank but also empty the ashtray, run the rubber floormats though a washer and wipe your front and rear windows with a damp cloth as well. All the while, you will be sitting in the petrol station's office, reading the newspaper provided or watching television. And there is no tip to pay at the end of it all.

'The Japanese understand the difference between giving service and being servile,' says Maire Brankin, a social anthropologist and management consultant who has lived in Japan. In the West, we tend to think of servants as doing a menial and unworthy job, but in Japan providing good service is a mark of pride in one's work and a source of respect from others. 'In Japan, the obligation to your customers is overwhelming,' says David Clifford of Dentsu's British associate company, Collett Dickenson Pearce. 'The philosophy of customer service is an all-consuming fixation. The customer is king, and there is fantastic loyalty to him. People see themselves as there to serve the customer.'

The quality of service that a customer receives from shops, from restaurants, from hotels and from every area of daily life is far higher than in Europe. This can create its own difficulties. The Japanese enthusiasm for packaging means that it is impossible to make a quick purchase in a department store, for example. You must have a perfectly wrapped product if you are to be seen carrying it in the street. The store has to maintain its reputation for service. This has two further consequences. Firstly, the pace of life on a shopping expedition has to be reduced. There is no point in thinking you can rush from shop to shop. Customer service takes time and the customer must take that time to receive the service. The second tangible consequence is that there is a good market in wrapping paper and other packaging materials. One of the merits of buying a gift at a prestigious department store is that the recipient will know from the wrapping paper that it was purchased at a top store, and that therefore you have attached great importance to the present. It would be cheaper, though, to buy the same gift at a supermarket or a discount store, and then wrap it yourself in best department store paper. Thus was born the lively market, especially at the gift-giving seasons, in department store wrapping paper. The paper is not, of course, sold by the store whose name is on it: it is sold by street traders and tiny corner shops who understand what the customer really wants. After all, the customer is king.

Dentsu, the advertising and media-buying giant, states that 'very attractive packaging is a must for successful entry into the Japanese market.' The success of Jardines Wines and Spirits confirms this. A crucial part of their success has been the style and shape of their packaging, which in many cases is quite different from the international packaging for the same product. The Virgin Megastore sells a high percentage of Japanese locally packaged compact discs which cost up to 20 per cent more than the imported product. The sound is identical, but they are more acceptable to the local population because of their packaging. The packaging of the store itself, with high ceilings and individual listening booths, is a further ingredient in its attraction for the Japanese public.

Many companies, when looking at the Japan market, will realise very quickly that, because of labelling requirements under Japanese law, there will have to be some changes to their domestic labels, even if it is only to add the correct form of Japanese wording as a product description. It would be very sensible to take the opportunity to review the entire package for its suitability for Japan. Are the colours right? Is the shape right? Is the name right? Is the size right? As Dentsu says, 'Appearance must also be perfect. Packaging should reflect the high quality and care a company puts into its product.' You may end up with an entirely different product for the Japanese market, but it will at least be one that sells.

As a sideline to the packaging question, but one that can affect the level of success a product achieves in Japan, it is worth considering the impact of your product name there. Most big-selling foreign products use the brand name by which they are known internationally. This is generally the right policy. The Japanese are very brand conscious, and if Rolls Royce, for example, had decided to change their name because it had too many 'r's and 'l's to make it easy for the Japanese to pronounce, there is no doubt the sales would have been affected. The Japanese actually seem to take pride in coming up with names for domestic products which they find difficult to pronounce. Among the models of car on sale in Japan are the Corolla, the Gloria and the Laurel, all hard for a Japanese to pronounce, as are other words like Walkman and Camcorder that have slipped into the English language from Japan. On the other hand, any brand name with too many sounds that are foreign to the Japanese language, such as the 'th' sound, or diphthong vowels, may pose too great a problem and, just as British people have had trouble with Japanese names such as Mitsubishi and Matsushita, so the Japanese consumer may be shy about asking for a product he or she is unsure about pronouncing correctly.

Advertising and the Agencies

At the heart of Japanese marketing, sales promotion and advertising are the advertising agencies, such as Dentsu and Hakuhodo. They are more than just advertising agencies in the way we know them in the West, and their influence on Japanese business is immense.

Dentsu began as a news agency, and grew into advertising on the theory that if they were supplying news to the media, why not supply advertising as well? 'The oligopolistic strength of Dentsu is accounted for by its relationship with the media,' says David Clifford. 'It is now by far the biggest media planning and buying agency in the world. It has a huge share of some television channels' advertising time, perhaps 60 per cent or more.' The total figures are overwhelming. As Table 4 shows, the advertising expenditure in Japan in 1990 was ¥5 564 800 million (say £24 000 million), of which Dentsu's share was about 24 per cent and Hakuhodo's 12 per cent. 'But I do not trust the figures,' says Clifford. 'In real terms, excluding classified advertising and semi-displays, it must be higher than that.' Dentsu claims a gross income of $1316 million in 1989, on billings of $10 063 million, figures which put them well ahead of second-placed Saatchi & Saatchi as the largest agency in the world. In fact, their billings were two-thirds as much again as those of Saatchi & Saatchi. Hakuhodo were tenth on the world-wide list, with billings of $4449

Table 4: Advertising Expenditures by Media

Medium	Advertising Expenditures (Unit: ¥ billions)			Percentage Growth	Percentage of Total
	1988	1989	1990	1990	1990
Newspapers	1126.7	1272.5	1359.2	+6.8	24.5
Magazines	296.2	335.4	374.1	+11.5	6.7
Radio	187.9	208.4	233.5	+12.0	4.2
Television	1316.1	1462.7	1604.6	+9.7	28.8
Sales Promotion	1482.8	1783.0	1981.5	+11.1	35.6
New Media	7.8	9.5	11.9	+25.3	0.2
Total	4415.5	5071.5	5564.8	+9.7	100.0

Note: *'Sales Promotion' includes Direct Mail, Flyers, Posters, Telephone Directories, Exhibitions, Point-of-purchase advertisements, Transit (railways, subways, etc). 'New Media' includes Cable TV, satellite TV and teletext services*

(Source: Dentsu, 1991)

million, not quite half those of Dentsu. There were four other Japanese agencies in the top 30, Tokyu, Dai-ichi Kikaku, Daiko and Asatsu, but their combined billings were less than Hakuhodo's. It is easy to understand that the big two agencies have what amounts to a stranglehold on the Japanese advertising industry.

Dentsu and Hakuhodo operate in a different world from the big Western agencies. Dentsu have 3000 clients, but for only about one-third of them do they undertake creative work. For the rest of their clients, they act purely as media buyers. 'The company is run by media buyers,' says Clifford. 'Of 6000 employees, only 1000 are creative. In Collett Dickenson Pearce or any major Western agency, perhaps one in three is creative.' The agencies also cope quite easily with clients who are promoting competitive products. They do this by having separate offices for separate accounts. Dentsu has perhaps 20 or 30 different offices in Tokyo alone, and they avoid conflict of interest by trying to ensure that the teams handling the different accounts never come into contact with each other. They are far more likely to meet Hakuhodo people working on another aspect of the same client's account than Dentsu people working on a competitive one. 'Clients choose agencies on account of their buying power,' says Hiromi Yoshida of Dentsu. 'Agencies are media buyers first and the creative side is added later. So it is not unusual, for example, for Hakuhodo to do the creative work and for Dentsu to do the media buying, but the connection between Hakuhodo and Dentsu is only through the client. There is no close direct relationship.'

It is equally true that there is a strong dislike of interlopers. The American corporate raider T. Boone Pickens, in the middle of his fight to gain control of Koito, wanted to place advertisements to tell other shareholders about the situation within Koito and of his bid to buy the company. He was told by the advertising agencies that there was no media space available, and that there never would be.

The iron hand with which the big agencies seem to control the Japanese advertising world does not prevent other ideas and other agencies from flourishing. Japan is the second biggest market in the world for advertising expenditure, after the United States, although it spends a slightly lower percentage of its GNP on advertising than is spent in Britain. Most of the major foreign agencies are active in Tokyo, the biggest being McCann Erickson, who have major international clients in Japan like Coca-Cola, American Express and Exxon. However, most agencies have come to Japan in a tie-up with a Japanese agency. So, for example, McCann Erickson has a joint venture with Hakuhodo, and Young & Rubicam operates in Japan through a tie-up with Dentsu. The only independently successful advertising agency in Japan has been J. Walter Thompson, a wholly owned part of the British conglomerate WPP. Ogilvy & Mather is not in Japan at all. 'Many American clients began with their American agency when they first came to Japan,' says Yoshida, 'but when they are really serious, they tend to move their account to Dentsu or Hakuhodo. It is no problem to handle competing accounts. We handle all the major Japanese car makers, as well as BMW, Mercedes Benz, Peugeot and Jaguar.' But Yoshida confirms that Dentsu executives do not have everything their own way. 'Our major clients use rival agencies to encourage competition, so our account executives have to visit their clients every day so as not to be overtaken unexpectedly by a competitor. To foreigners, it may look as though Dentsu controls everything, but actually, an account executive's life is very competitive.'

There are a number of perceived unchangeable laws of marketing and advertising in Japan which are frequently quoted. However, they are more honoured in the breach than the observance. It is said, for example, that the Japanese do not like long-running advertising campaigns such as the British public enjoy, like British Telecom's Beattie campaign, or the Brooke Bond chimps. 'Japanese clients and consumers want constant change. This is completely against the received Western wisdom that brands are built by consistency over time,' argues David Clifford. 'I can only think of two such long-running campaigns,' says Yoshida. 'There is one for Nescafé Gold Blend, and another for the vitamin drink, Ripobitan.' This is a good example of the Japanese assumption that if it is not the accepted practice, it cannot exist. In reality, there are plenty of successful long-running campaigns in Japan. 'Our 13–year campaign for Hennessy cognac still works,' says Mark Bedingham of Jardines Wines & Spirits. Chris McDonald, Managing Director of Rolex (Japan) Ltd, says that Rolex is probably a better-known name in Tokyo than in Britain. 'That is largely because of our long-running celebrity testimonial campaign. We only ask people who have really made it in Japan, people like the polar explorer Naomi Uemura or the entertainer Yoko Morishita. And it works.'

There are examples of advertising campaigns on television, in newspapers and on the subways for the same product at the same time, all featuring different images and different consumer targeting because the three campaigns were being handled independently by three different agencies. This takes the idea that the Japanese want constant change to what would seem to us to be a ridiculous extreme, but it works. The general rule of Japanese advertising is that change is good and that long-running campaigns do not work – but there are many examples of the successful use of the latter.

Using foreign images in advertising is certainly common. Many *gaijin* residents of Tokyo supplement their income, or their children's pocket money, by modelling for products from wedding dresses to restaurants, and there are many professional non-Japanese models earning a fortune in Japan. For some time, the Princess of Wales was the most saleable face to put on the front of a women's magazine in Japan, and emphasising the foreign origin of a consumer product is usually a key selling point. 'It is natural in clothes and fashion to use foreign models,' says Hiromi Yoshida. 'That trend has been adapted for other products, too. But we would not normally use blonde models for traditional Japanese products, like *sake* or *kimono*.'

Foreign product names are also usual in Japan. We have already noted car names like Gloria and Laurel (two Nissan brand names that are only used within Japan), but the use of foreign names is widespread across the complete spectrum of consumer goods. They vary from internationally accepted brands like National, Citizen and Sharp to more obscure Japanese products which could not possibly succeed without a change of product name. Who would buy a health drink called Pocari Sweat in Britain? Or a brand of cigarettes called Hope? The art of spotting, and laughing at, prime examples of 'Japlish' in the magazines and streets of Tokyo is a favourite foreigners' hobby, but it needs to be put in context. Yes, there are cheap laughs to be gained from an advertising slogan like 'Nice Tool, Nice Life' (for a range of gardening equipment), but the point is that it works for the local market.

Misuse of English in Japan is no more common than the misuse of Japanese is in Europe. Japanese characters written back to front or upside-down are reasonably common in Western advertising, but because most Europeans only recognise the image of Japan that a character represents, and not the character itself, nobody really minds whether the character has been written correctly. The same is true of the use of foreign languages in Japan. Foreign words have a glamour that sells. It is not the word itself that is important, it is the message it conveys.

'When foreign companies first come here they do not really appreciate Japanese ideas,' says Yoshida. 'Advertisements in Japan often have no apparent relevance to the product at all, and Western companies want relevance. But irrelevance can work. For example, the Parco fashion retail stores used a campaign comprising many completely irrelevant advertisements, but they were always stylish, and they built an innovative image for Parco. Their competitors could not do the same thing.

'Television advertisements are not there to persuade consumers. They are there to make a noise in the market-place. To create awareness, you need a strong impact, but the meaning of the strong impact in Japan is different from in Britain. For example, you do not need to use wit to grab the audience's attention. In Japan, we tend to use noise. Of course, humour can sell in Japan. In that sense, Japan is different from the United States. What British people and the Japanese have in common is that we do not like to be sold to. But you cannot be too subtle, because the next commercial will drown out the time the consumer is thinking about your message.'

A great deal of Japanese advertising is corporate image advertising, aimed at promoting an image rather than a specific product. Dentsu, who handle practically all the sports sponsorship in Japan, believe they have been successful in that field because it links in with the need to sell on the basis of company name rather than product image. 'For the same reason, there are enormous neon signs in Ginza with just a company name. Japanese corporations consider this a very effective means of advertising.' Yoshida believes that this type of advertising will grow significantly in future. 'Tennis players with advertising logos on their shirts – that began in Japan. We believe in a co-ordination of all the media under our "Total Communication" theme. If Steffi Graf, for example, would wear a company's logo on her shirt, and appear on a television advertisement and perhaps a billboard with just the company name and no other message, it would work. And it does not matter whether the product is coffee or computers. The message is that she is the best and this is the best.'

Public Relations

The Japanese do not have a reputation for good public relations. They come off second best in the international arguments over trade, whaling, economic imperialism and sexual tourism to name but a few; and the very definition of the Japanese as inscrutable and impossible to understand implies little success in their attempts to get their international message across. This does not mean, though, that public relations is an underdeveloped art in Japan.

According to Dentsu Burson-Marsteller, the public relations arm of the oligopoly, 'The most significant issue in international business today is the relationship between Japan and the Western economies.

Foreign companies seeking commercial links in Japan face exceptional communications challenges.' Corporate public relations is conducted in several directions at once, and the different strands need to be identified by any corporation looking to get its message across successfully in Japan. Firstly, there is what the Japanese call 'corporate communications'. This involves the way the company relates to the community at large and the way it promotes its image as a good citizen. Horror stories such as that of the Chisso company, which was finally forced out of business by the outcry against Minamata disease, a crippling condition caused by Chisso's dumping of mercury and other chemicals into the local water supply, are engraved on the hearts of corporate public relations officers. They are very much aware of the power of the local community, and all Japanese companies now try to play a positive leading role in its affairs. Companies no longer are content to be known for the excellence of their balance sheet: they also want to be respected for their social conscience.

Investor relations is the second arm of Japanese corporate public relations. Letting your shareholders know about the company is becoming more important as Japanese firms become more international in their scope, and making sure that investors are proud of the company they have placed their faith and their money in is a vital cog in the PR machine. However, perhaps the most crucial role being played these days by PR staff is in internal communications, to ensure better understanding by employees of the way their company is working, and to maintain and improve staff morale. If the work-force is a crucial asset of the company, retaining employees and making them ever more efficient is a full-time job for the PR departments. Today they are increasingly involved in strategic planning.

Most major Japanese companies have a great deal of promotional material printed in English, and British companies in Japan need obviously to have material available in Japanese to explain their own activities to the local market. The Japanese have a devouring interest in written and statistical material about any organisation relevant to them, and this interest must be satisfied.

There is no doubt that it is absolutely essential to understand the options open for your particular product message, and to use them to the full. Mark Bedingham of Jardines identifies the need to continue to persuade shareholders that a high level of profit reinvestment in advertising is crucial to their success as one of his main challenges for the future. Jardines have one of their major accounts with a Japanese agency, and two other big accounts with American agencies. 'We will continue to accelerate our advertising and promotional spend, so that for our leading brands we are investing at levels similar to domestic competition. We take a brand-by-brand approach. All our advertising is created in Japan, either by Western agencies employing Japanese staff, or by a Japanese agency. But whichever way we create it, it must go through the disciplines of Western marketing.'

Tokyo and Osaka – The Great Divide

Most of what has been written so far has been based on the views of people living in Tokyo, watching the market there, and yet everyone is agreed that Osaka, the second city 500 kilometres (310 miles) south-west of Tokyo, is a completely different market. 'They speak a completely different language and they think differently', says Hiromi Yoshida. 'Their way of joking is completely different. An Osaka person is more Italian in his sense of humour, more direct. In Tokyo we are more British. We produce different television advertisements for Tokyo and Osaka. For example, for a recent horror movie, the ad for Tokyo was understated, but for Osaka we had to show the bloodiest scenes to appeal to the consumer.'

They do not, of course, speak a completely different language in Osaka. But they do have a strong regional accent, and a vocabulary of local dialect words which make the Osaka language as different from Tokyo's as Liverpool's is, for example, from the Queen's English. The main difference is not in the language or in the apparent blood-thirstiness of the Osaka resident; it is in his dedication to business.

This has a historical basis which should not be underestimated. 'In the Tokugawa period, from 1603 to 1868,' says Ryosuke Wada, President of Wadatetsu KK and a pillar of the Osaka business community, 'all the regions of Japan sold their products through Osaka. All the *daimyo* (feudal lords) had their warehouses in Nakanoshima in the centre of Osaka. In Tokyo, the population was 80 per cent samurai and 20 per cent merchants. In Osaka it was the other way around. This was the key point. Osaka has always been a merchants' city and Tokyo the government city.' The common greeting in Osaka is still, '*Mo karimakka?*' which, being translated, roughly means, 'Are you making money?' The reply is often a straightforward, '*Mo karahen*' ('No. I'm not).

The concept of the Osaka merchant is still very strong in Japan, especially in Osaka itself, where they are proud of their trade background. Osaka itself was founded in AD 578, while Tokyo is a city that began to grow only four hundred years ago, so to the Osaka people Tokyo is an upstart. The people of west Japan (Kansai, as opposed to Kanto – east Japan) are more like the Chinese in their business manners than their less effusive Tokyo cousins. 'They are able to take quicker decisions; they are much more positive; they don't beat about the bush,' believes Gordon Williams, formerly British Consul-General in Osaka. 'But they are still Japanese in their style.' Yet, on the whole, the Osaka consumer's taste is more conservative. In Tokyo they seize upon the latest fads and fashions, so that products may have a life cycle of months rather than years. In Osaka they are more faithful to their favourite products.

Many of the major merchant houses of today began in Osaka, as did several of the banks and many of the biggest manufacturing companies. Of the major trading companies, C. Itoh, Sumitomo and Marubeni all began in Osaka, as did retailers like Takashimaya and Daiei. The Sumitomo Bank, the Sanwa Bank and the Daiwa Bank are all Osaka-based, as are the manufacturers Matsushita, Sanyo and Sharp. The rivalry between the Osaka company Matsushita and the Tokyo company Sony is exaggerated as much by their different geographical origins as by their product competitiveness. There are still consumers in Tokyo who will not buy a National product because it comes from the Kansai, and there are Osaka customers who will not buy a Tokyo-made Sony product.

Osaka today is a thriving international city with a population of about 5 million. The six prefectures that officially make up the Kansai region, Osaka, Wakayama, Nara, Shiga, Kyoto and Hyogo, have a combined population of 21 million, and account for 3 per cent of the world's GNP. The region is also the centre of some of the most ambitious construction projects in the world. The Kansai International Airport, built on reclaimed land in Osaka Bay, opened in September 1994 at a cost of 'approximately ¥1 trillion for the construction of the airport island and ¥2.5 trillion for related regional development'. A new coastal bay road, stretching 60 kilometres from the new airport to the port city of Kobe and beyond, will cost another ¥1.22 trillion, although the monorail from the airport will be cheaper, at only ¥105 billion. Another ¥1 trillion will be spent on the bridges linking the islands of Honshu and Shikoku via Awaji at the entrance to the Inland Sea, and, perhaps the most ambitious project of them all, the Kansai Science City, will consume an initial estimate of ¥3 trillion before it is completed early in the next century. According to the Centre for the Industrial Renovation of the Kansai, ¥40.2 trillion will ultimately be invested in the 882 projects scheduled for completion before the end of this century. Osaka is not a place to be ignored.

If there is rivalry between Tokyo and Osaka, there is also, to a greater or lesser extent, rivalry between Tokyo and all other parts of Japan. The great technological revolution, which was to have decentralised the population because the need to meet would disappear when computers could link us up electronically, has, in fact, created an even greater centralising role for Tokyo. As Takamitsu Sawa, Professor of Economics at Kyoto University, pointed out at the Toshiba International Foundation conference on Technological Innovation and Society in London at the end of 1991, 'It seems that one in every four Japanese now lives in the Tokyo area. In an information-centred society, information becomes extremely valuable, and financial information can become the source of great wealth. Nevertheless, information is valuable only when it is possessed by few people: information that is known by everyone is worthless. Consequently the information that flows through information networks may be deemed to be "spoiled knowledge", of minimal value.' His theory is that because information from abroad generally comes to Japan through Tokyo, and over 90 per cent of Japan's news is broadcast from Tokyo, anyone wanting 'high-priced' information must go to Tokyo frequently, and any company hoping to gain similarly valuable information must establish an office in Tokyo. 'As a result, people and companies gather in Tokyo with no end to the process in sight. The new information network spread across the face of Japan, which at first seemed to promise precisely the opposite, has caused people to come to Tokyo to gather precious information through the primitive technique of face-to-face meetings. The dining-places and nightclubs of Ginza and Akasaka have become the prime sites of information exchange.'

The dining-places and night-clubs of Osaka and Kobe, of Fukuoka and Sapporo, of Nagoya and Hiroshima are also places of information exchange, and the residents of those cities would argue strongly that to do business in Japan, you should look beyond Tokyo. The uncomfortable truth, however, is that unless you have particular projects to aim at in other parts of Japan, you can succeed in most of your marketing aims without moving out of Tokyo. You will not enjoy yourself half as much, but from a business point of view, practically everything can be achieved from a Tokyo base.

Hilton Hotels – A Case History

'When the Ladbroke Group bought Hilton Hotels from the Allegis Corporation in October 1987, the only thing that changed significantly was our sales and marketing policy,' says Geoffrey Breeze, Hilton's Corporate Vice-president – Marketing. 'Of course, the British took over the top management positions as well.'

The Hilton Hotel in Tokyo had for many years been one of the leading hotels for foreigners in Japan, with a dominant position in central Tokyo, and a reputation for its restaurants and its ability to put on the best functions which made it very popular with the local foreign community. In the early 1980s, however, there was a parting of the ways between Hilton and its Japanese partner. The old Hilton became the Capitol Tokyu Hotel. By 1984, a new Tokyo Hilton had been built in Shinjuku, and many of the management and staff moved with the hotel. It continued with the old Hilton's reputation for excellent food and a banqueting service second to none, but because it was less central, and because a large number of new international hotels were built in Tokyo in the 1980s, it lost some of its reputation as a purely foreign hotel. Now only about 35 per cent of its guests are foreigners, with Americans the largest single sector. In Japan, the Hilton is not perceived as a British hotel. Even the British are sometimes surprised to learn where the ownership lies.

'There are not enough hotel rooms in Tokyo,' according to Hiroshi Nakamura, Resident Manager of the Tokyo Hilton. 'We routinely have occupancy rates in the high 80 per cents. All the same, our income is about one-third from our banqueting operation, one-third from restaurants and bars, and just the remaining one-third from rooms.'

When Ladbroke took over the Hilton hotels the longstanding manager of the Tokyo Hilton, Richard Handl, was able to make a few improvements in the way the group looked at its Japanese customers. The number of Japanese guests staying world-wide in Hilton hotels has grown to such an extent that in 1992 they will form the largest single national group of guests, taking more than one-fifth of all Hilton rooms. The Hilton group now has more hotels in Japan, in Osaka, Tokyo Bay and Nagoya. 'Our investment in Japan was the starting-point for real success there,' says Breeze. 'While we had only one hotel, we were perceived as a foreigners' hotel. But now, for example, our Tokyo Bay hotel, next to Disneyland, is totally orientated towards Japanese holiday-makers. Our Nagoya hotel is for Japanese businessmen. We are a foreign brand, but in Japan we are for the Japanese more than for the foreigner.'

Hilton have developed a world-wide marketing approach which they call '*Wa no kutsurogi*', which, very roughly, means, 'Making yourself at home, the Japanese way'. Geoffrey Breeze says it gives comfort and security, as defined by the Hilton's Japanese guests. 'We have de-emphasised the hotelier approach and emphasised the customer approach. Forget the slippers and the green tea. That's easy. That's what everybody does. We looked further, at the fire instructions which were only written in English. That did not make a Japanese guest feel at home. We make sure, too, that analogue alarm clocks are provided for every room used by a Japanese guest. If he cannot speak very good English he will be shy about booking an alarm call in a foreign country, so we give him an alarm clock, to make him feel more at home.'

Within Japan, Hilton have followed a consistent approach, but not necessarily one that has been based entirely on Japanese rules. International marketing precepts work in Japan just as they do elsewhere. The language may be different, but good marketing makes sense everywhere. 'Our reputation and product experience allowed us to raise prices very considerably domestically,' says Breeze. This policy is supported not only by continuing high occupancy rates, but also by Hiroshi Nakamura's assertion that, 'Price is not a question as long as our guest gets value for money.'

Breeze believes, like many others in many different businesses, that success in Japan has had a significant impact on their success elsewhere. 'Our re-emphasis on the domestic market in Japan really made the difference. At that stage we had not been in competition with domestic chains, and, unlike our foreign competition, we did not charge Americans the earth and discount to the Japanese – we did just about the opposite, if anything. The appreciation of the yen forced us into looking at the domestic market seriously, but we would have done so anyway. We coupled this with re-emphasising our ethnic restaurants, the Hilton Club and our private dining-clubs within the hotel such as the Golden Key Club in Shinjuku.' There are also two Rotary Clubs and three Lions Clubs which meet at the Tokyo Hilton, with 99 per cent Japanese membership. 'Hilton is still perceived in Japan as an American brand, and we make no attempt to change that perception. Outside Japan, we are almost perceived by Japanese guests as a Japanese brand.'

The British hands-on style of management that Ladbroke brought to the Hilton in Japan has changed their Japanese managers' lives. 'It used to be poor form for a senior manager to talk to junior staff,' says Breeze, 'but now all members of staff, at whatever level, talk directly to each other on subjects that concern them.'

'Here at the Hilton,' confirms Hiroshi Nakamura, 'we have a visible management. We spend only 10 per cent of our working hours in the office, and the rest of the time out and about in the hotel, talking with staff and guests, and checking guest rooms and restaurants.' However, he also points out the cultural difficulties of Management By Walking About. 'Most Japanese cannot say "no" to a senior person. If something goes wrong, the junior will be blamed, so he will not argue with a superior. In the West, you have meetings to make decisions. In Japan, we have meetings to discuss a problem.'

In Geoffrey Breeze's view, the *Wa no Kutsurogi* programme is important as a marketing initiative because it emphasises the partnership between the hotel and its guests. 'The customers define the quality standards, and each hotel wanting to take part in the service must invite local Japanese business agents to approve the standards offered. Even if *Wa no Kusurogi* fails as a consumer service, it would have succeeded because of the partnership it has built with major trade distributors.'

Direct Marketing

'Direct marketing is dangerous for us in Japan,' says Breeze, 'because we do not have the opportunity to understand with whom we are doing business.' The received wisdom is that direct marketing, mail-shots and the like, cannot work in Japan because it bypasses the important stage of relationship building. Certainly, it is true that Japan has historically been far slower to develop its mail order business than most economically advanced nations.

However, the fact remains that direct mail advertising outlays in 1990 hit the ¥200 billion mark. Almost two billion pieces of advertising mail were delivered. Mail order and credit companies continue their robust attacks on the market, and in recent years there has also been a revision in prices for bulk-order mailshots, thanks to the introduction of new systems for handling high-volume mailings. According to the Japan Mail Order Sales Association figures, total sales by mail-order firms have doubled in five years and now stand at around ¥1.5 trillion (say £9.3 billion). 'It used to be that the Japanese consumer wanted to see the goods first,' says Gordon Williams in Osaka. 'But now, because good savings can be made by mail order, such business is growing.' Banks and finance houses are using direct mailshots increasingly, and a new joint venture between Sun Alliance and a major Japanese insurance firm, to sell insurance on a direct-marketing basis, has recently been worked out. The future prospects for mail order in Japan are very good, spurred on not only by changes in the postal rates but also by the massive cost of land for retail premises in Japan. Department stores are among the leading agencies in developing mail-order business to extend their penetration without having to build new stores on land that, in places, is valued higher than gold dust.

Successful Marketing

There is no magic answer to the problems of marketing in Japan. There are only guidelines that have worked for other people. Retaining the Britishness of the image is usually a good idea. 'We made no changes to the retailing style of Marui, except our image,' says Mike Inman of Virgin Megastore. 'In terms of record retailing, that's new. We believe you have to adapt to suit the country you are in but also to bring in what is strong and unique to you. What we are selling is the framework: the product itself is not unique to Virgin. So to do exactly as you would overseas is not only wrong but also impracticable. You couldn't find a building like our Paris store, with sweeping staircases and chandeliers, in Japan anyway.'

Akira Nakamura, Virgin Atlantic Airways' Vice-president – Japan, believes that success begins with corporate goals. 'There is no success in Japan if a company has no concept. All corporations who succeed in Japan have a clear concept. Our concept was that we are not an airline. We not only carry passengers, we want to give them enjoyment. We are a consumer-oriented carrier. We always look at the market from our passengers' viewpoint. So our advertising never includes aircraft or an exotic girl smiling at the passengers. For all British companies, the concept is vital. If the concept appeals to the Japanese public, then success is assured.'

CHAPTER 8

NEGOTIATING WITH THE JAPANESE

'We go into a meeting and there are maybe two of us, and there are often six or seven of them, and of those maybe two will actually say anything. We sit there for half a hour sucking our teeth. For me that was a big cultural shock when I first came here, but now I am quite used to it.' Mike Inman of Virgin Megastore's views on the abstruse arts of negotiation with the Japanese are echoed by almost every foreigner in Japan. Inman continues: 'When I first came here we had to re-invent everything. We had to break everything down in meetings and discuss why is a rack square, why is a compact disc round? We are theorising about everything, large groups of people in small rooms with everybody chain-smoking. You come out at about 11 o'clock at night, six hours of bashing your head against the table, really just confirming what you came in with, and you think, what's the point of it all? But it's all education, it is all building up knowledge.'

'You will get two groups of people going into the same meeting, Europeans and Japanese,' says Dr George Newns of British Telecom. 'After two hours, the Europeans come out saying, "Great, we've got a deal." The Japanese come out saying, "What was all that about?" You need somebody there to interpret the signs and the body language as much as the words that are spoken.'

Negotiating with the Japanese is considered by most who have had any contact with Japan to be the most difficult of the local business arts to master. 'In negotiations, the kernel of truth is hard to fish out,' says Ben Thorne, formerly Commercial Counsellor at the British Embassy, and now a consultant on Japan trade. Understanding why the Japanese are negotiating with you, and realising what they really want to gain from the deal being discussed is the key to success. This is, I suppose, self-evident and would apply to negotiations with any other nationality or interest group anywhere in the world. However, the Japanese may feel the need to hide the true motive for a negotiation more thoroughly than a European will, and the search for what is really going on can be more difficult than in other negotiations. Of course, it does not follow that the motive behind a business deal is not exactly what it appears to be on the surface. The Japanese do, as we have seen, make the distinction between *tatemae* (face) and *honne* (true intentions), but often they are one and the same thing.

Sitting by the Window

'A lot of Japanese negotiations are negative,' says Thorne. 'They feel it is rude to tell a foreign visitor they do not want to do business with his company, so they negotiate their way towards a "no".' There is a category of worker in any Japanese company of any size, known as *madogiwazoku*. This translates roughly as, 'the chap who sits by the window'. Within a Japanese corporation there are inevitably people who cannot climb all the way to the top of the hierarchy, but they are not pushed out of the corporate structure simply because they have outlived their usefulness.

These people sit by the window and become window-watchers. Their function internally is to look out of the window all day and check that the trees outside are still in the same place as yesterday, or to ensure that nobody has stolen the car park. In between times, they still attend internal meetings, answer the telephone and drink their share of *ocha*, but their colleagues know they are no longer key members of the organisation, even if they themselves do not. Their business cards will still identify them by their rank within the hierarchy, so there is no way of telling from a first meeting whether the company representative that you have been dealing with is one of the *madogiwazoku* or not.

Because the window people are basically useless, and are therefore a cost rather than an asset, few are based outside Japan, working for Japanese companies in Britain, for example. However, in Japan they have one task which they perform successfully. That is to give an enthusiastically polite reception to a visiting *gaijin* without committing the company in any way. If you arrive for a first meeting with a Japanese corporation, and if you do not have a solid basis for discussion, it may well be that you will be faced first of all by one of the window people. He will assure you that, yes, his company is indeed interested in your widgets, and the price of £100 each, which is only four times the local market price, certainly seems very reasonable. After all, you know that price is not the only factor in negotiating with the Japanese. Perhaps a six-month delivery is a little long when compared with the ex-stock terms offered by all your competitors, but he would assure you that this is a minor problem that can be overcome. So can the slight quality set-back you have experienced in all other export markets where every third widget falls apart on being removed from its frankly tatty box.

The *madogiwazoku* will assure you that progress is being made, but it is not. The only way to avoid wasting hours dealing with such a person is to plan your meetings well in advance, and make sure that you research the company and its personnel first. Do not turn up uninvited: you will get nowhere. Make sure that you have an introduction, the essential basis for a relationship, and that your company really has something to offer in the deal. If not, all you will be able to do on your return to the office is write a wonderful and detailed report on the reception you received, which will be read with admiration by all your superiors until they realise what response there has been to your follow-up letters and faxes. None at all.

Negotiation Styles

Doing business in Japan, as we have already seen, requires patience, and the need for patience is never more obvious than when setting out on a negotiation. The Japanese style when negotiating with their fellow-countrymen is to find a win-win position, so that both sides genuinely feel they have got something positive out of the deal. The Japanese view is that if both sides are not equally happy with the deal, it will soon founder, and all the effort put into creating it will have been wasted.

The Western style of negotiation is more close to a win-lose ideal. The difference in emphasis comes from the Western belief in absolutes, that there must be a right answer and we must find it, compared with the Japanese trust in relativity, that there is no right answer only the best one. In a Western negotiation, one side ends up with the right answer and one side with the wrong one. In Japan, the result that is being looked for is the best one, where neither side is wrong.

'When a Japanese negotiates in a Japanese setting, the ground rules are that a compromise must be achieved,' says Ben Thorne. 'But the good Japanese negotiator has also been taught that foreigners do not compromise. So when dealing with foreigners, he may well be looking for a 100 per cent victory.' He adds an interesting word of warning, which makes the game of negotiation poker even more complicated: 'Do not try to learn Japanese ways, as the Japanese have already learnt your ways. If you deal with them in what you perceive to be a Japanese way, and they are dealing with you in what they perceive to be a Western way, then neither side will understand the other.' 'However right you think you have got it,' adds Rosemary Yates of Sheffield University, 'they will move the goalposts.'

'You need to understand why they behave in a way we think odd,' says Yates. 'Do not be Japanese, just know what makes them tick.' She tells the story of a British businessman who, on a visit to Japan, said to his Japanese opposite number, 'Since I last saw you, my wife has died.' The Japanese reaction was laughter. It was not a callous laugh but an embarrassed one. The Japanese did not know how to react to a Westerner under those circumstances, and instinctively laughed to cover his discomfiture.

'Japanese capitalism in many senses has no relation to Western capitalism,' believes Thorne, 'which often makes their goal hard for us to understand. For example, they tend not to look for dividends early on, but rather plough back the profits into a new venture.' The Japanese will always have a goal for their negotiations when they start, but are in many ways more flexible than Westerners in reaching the best achievable conclusion, rather than the only correct conclusion. It is important to identify at the outset what are likely to be the crucial points in any negotiation. For example, price is unlikely to be the key factor in a negotiation concerning consumer goods. Of much more importance will be the quality and image presented. Bob Pearce of Cornes believes that, 'Price is not the benchmark. You need to convince one or two people in one or two outlets that the product has quality.' On the other hand, with industrial products, price can be of the utmost importance. 'All this rubbish about a product lasting 15 years does not matter. Japanese production techniques change so rapidly that your product will be obsolete well before then anyway. You need a product with a shorter lifetime but at a lower price.'

'Do not waste your time on a product the Japanese cannot use,' advises Dick Large of British Aerospace. This means that you have to identify how the customer needs to use the product before you get into too much negotiation. Do not assume that it will be used in Japan in the same way as in other countries. Many a manufacturer has seen his hopes founder on that assumption. 'And make sure they can get the product. If the distribution system cannot get the product to the market, the best negotiated deal is of no value.'

It is essential that you understand what makes your Japanese partner tick. Hiroshi Mikami of Japan Medico made a deal for Portex products many years ago which was based around delivery. 'At the beginning, Portex delivery was awful. I eventually said, "I will pay more than other markets, provided I get the best service." Since then, things have gone very well, even though I know I pay more than most other markets for my products.'

A Japanese negotiator will not move a long way from the starting-point: usually there is little movement on the basics of price, delivery and quality. The idea of haggling, of an opening position from which you are prepared to move significantly like an East End market trader offloading doubtful crockery, is something alien to the Japanese way of negotiation, and they do not respect people who use these tactics. 'However well you prepare for your negotiations,' says Ben Thorne, 'your Japanese opposite numbers will have prepared better.' They will know your true position before you begin. Their research will have identified what you can offer, so to exaggerate by giving, for example, inflated sales statistics for other parts of the world or exaggerated price information, will do you no good. The Japanese will not take anything you say as the accepted truth if it does not agree with their own research. They have little respect for people who begin their negotiations from an unrealistic point. They see this as merely a time-wasting exercise which diverts attention from getting to the real issues.

Time-wasting is not, however, a tactic that the Japanese despise. 'They will use you as a stalking horse,' says Andrew Lawson of the CBI. 'They will waste your time and pick your brains mercilessly.' Many negotiations seem to get bogged down in a series of meetings in which the Japanese find out a little more but the foreigners do not. The key word to keep remembering is patience, for, as Andrew Lawson says, 'The time eventually comes when they return the favour. But you have got to be prepared to wait.' No negotiation with the Japanese is totally wasted if you look upon it in the way they do, as an opportunity to build a relationship. This particular negotiation might fail, but you should have built up a reserve of goodwill and favours owed that can be called upon at a later date when the omens are more favourable.

'In a negotiation with a Westerner,' says Rosemary Yates, 'we are taught to keep up the aggression, to keep on talking to get our point across. With the Japanese, you have to take quite the opposite tack.

You must get them into the mode of drawing answers out of you, so that you appear modest.' In a Japanese meeting, it is quite common for there to be a long silence. Westerners, who are unsettled by an absence of words in a business discussion, will dive in with any old statement just to break their embarrassment. To the Japanese, silence is natural and they use it to consider what has just been said. The art is to make sure that it is they who break the silence, not you.

The Japanese style of rarely doing more than answering the question, and of being unwilling to venture information unless it has been specifically asked for, is something that a Westerner is well advised not only to be aware of but also to copy in his negotiations. The Japanese are very honest businessmen, and you will hear the truth and nothing but the truth from your Japanese counterparts. But you will not necessarily hear the whole truth, unless you have made sure by the way you phrase the question that it has come out. The Japanese language is vague, and you may need to ask the same question from three or four different angles before you are sure you have the answer you need.

We have already dealt with the importance of the Japanese language in business (see Chapter Two), and in crucial negotiations it is likely that the final deal will be concluded in English, which even the Japanese recognise as being more suitable for international agreements. As Malcolm Carlisle of Smiths Industries Medical Systems says of his joint venture negotiations with Kuraray, 'You should always contract under Japanese law, because it is pretty silly not to, but you make English the governing language. In practical terms, it is the only way to do it because the thought of having to translate into and out of Japanese all the time would be horrendous. It's a neat compromise. They get their legal system, you get your language.'

As with most joint venture discussions, the negotiations between SIMS and Kuraray were all in English. Only at the stage of the fine detail did the discussions switch to Japanese. 'English is increasingly an international language anyway. The points of principle would be made in English between ourselves and the other side, and then our lawyer, Hideshige Haruki of Braun Moriya Hoashi and Kubota, would argue if necessary in Japanese and present the arguments in more detail, but that's right at the end. The whole deal works in English, but at that stage you need a Japanese lawyer for several reasons. Firstly, because a detailed knowledge of the Japanese law is then essential. Secondly, because he's the man who will understand better the philosophy and approach of your Japanese partners in legal matters. And thirdly, because it is a level of detailed argument which is very difficult for the other side to conduct in English. It is unfair on them.'

International contracts with the Japanese are normally in English. Agreements between Swedish and Japanese companies, for example, have been written in English. Agreements between Japan and Brazil have also been in English, so it is not merely British arrogance that assumes everybody must speak our language at the crucial moment. As Nobufumi Kurita of JETRO points out, 'Contracts in English are better. English is logical and precise, but Japanese is not.'

Its imprecision is such that the Japanese *hai* means, as Humpty Dumpty said to Alice in *Through the Looking-Glass*, 'exactly what I wish (a word) to mean, no more and no less,' so the use of English in negotiations, with the aid of a professional legal interpreter, will not put you at a disadvantage.

An international agreement is bound to cross a language barrier, and English is a more commonly used business language than Japanese. To use it in negotiating an agreement is entirely reasonable. To use it when you are trying to sell something to a Japanese potential customer is, as we have seen in Chapter Two, somewhat tactless and sets up an unnecessary handicap. You would be unlikely to buy something from a Japanese person speaking Japanese in London, so why should the reverse case not also be true? However, major international partnership agreements are different, and any agreement which has English as its master language must also be negotiated in English.

The Negotiators

One of the disadvantages of a deal being negotiated in English is that everybody in head office assumes he is therefore qualified to negotiate. Putting a negotiating team together is an important task, and it should not be assumed that any semi-coherent person can qualify. A major part of the negotiation will be in building up the relationship between the two companies before any agreement is signed, rather than afterwards as might be the case in a purely European joint venture. Therefore, it is wrong to upstage your man in Japan, if you already have one, by excluding him from the team. If he is any good at all, he will have built up personal relationships which can only help the negotiations and he will have an understanding of how the Japanese are likely to think and react in given situations. If he is of no use to you in a negotiation, then what is he doing in Japan at all? Excluding your Tokyo resident from the team will only undermine his standing when the negotiations are over, and weaken your overall position in the market.

Yet it happens so often. The director of a firm which concluded a licence deal with a Japanese company says, 'We did not include our local man in the team that negotiated our agreement, because he is not an expert in the technical side of the business. This was a technical agreement.' If the negotiating team consisted of just one person, this might perhaps be a reasonable argument, but on the Japanese side there will be many people, several of whom will undertake roles in the negotiation that only become clear after many meetings, if at all. To include your local man in your team, even if all he does is sit in on meetings and be aware of what is going on, is, firstly, no inconvenience to your opposite numbers and, secondly, a confirmation to them that you need the advice of the man who is working for you on a permanent basis in Japan. It is also, of course, cheaper to have your local man in on the deal, even if it cuts across head office sensibilities or intrudes on divisional power bases. Running a negotiation in Japan will cost money, as does running an office there, so combining the two even slightly will relieve the financial burden a little.

Apart from your local man, who else should be on the team? Well, as the Japanese say, it is 'case by case'. You must always have a legal adviser available, and a fully briefed technical team to bring the necessary product knowledge to the table. Beyond that, it depends very much on the circumstances of the agreement, but where possible all members of the negotiating team should match the ideal profile for succeeding in Japan: they should have a long career with your company; they should be senior enough to carry weight but not too senior to force the negotiations on to a higher level than is practicable in Japan (i.e., no managing directors); and they should not have to work within a tight framework of preconditions or time-scale. They should all be aware of the need for the Japanese ideal win-win result rather than the win-lose outcome, which may be a success in Western terms but which will not result in any long-term partnership in Japan. As Rosemary Yates puts it, 'The only thing you need to know is the one thing you cannot teach – sensitivity.'

Visiting Firemen

As a slight side-track, it is worth recording the publicly stated views of the local representative of BMW, when he addressed a meeting of his Chamber of Commerce in Japan: 'One of the reasons that BMW have done so well in Japan is because we have had so few visits by our head office staff.' The remark produced much laughter from his audience, but the laughter was for the recognised truth behind his remarks. The BMW man went on to report that only his chairman, the head of engineering and the head of marketing are allowed to come to Japan except under exceptional circumstances. Most of his audience marvelled at his luck in having such a clear run and his skill at keeping his head office staff to this strict discipline.

Ask any businessman based in Tokyo what his main problems are, and you can be sure that 'dealing with head office' comes very high on the list. Head office includes those who like to visit Japan either to buy the latest electronic gadgets to take home, or to stay in a really luxurious hotel or to do both. If a couple of gladhanding visits have to be made to local businesses to justify the trip, this can easily be arranged by our man on the spot in between the shopping he can organise, and just before he runs the exhausted visiting fireman all the way back to Narita airport.

This is no longer acceptable. 'The days of the visitors who swan through Japan are long gone,' says Graham Harris of Lloyds Bank. 'We tell anybody who says he wants to visit a Japanese bank in Tokyo that he ought to visit their London office first, to establish the relationship and set up an agenda for a Tokyo meeting. If a chap comes all the way to Tokyo and visits, say, the Sumitomo Bank, the first question he is going to be asked is when did he last see their Mr Watanabe or whoever in London. The Sumitomo man is going to think it very odd if the reply is that he has never met their man in London. This tends to sort out the people who are really serious about coming to Japan.'

However, in a major company, it is the chief executive who sets the tone, so those are the visits that matter. 'It takes no effort for a chief executive to be quoted as saying "Japan is important to us" in the newspapers. It is a lot more effort actually to come here.' Harris is lucky in that his chairman visits Japan on a regular basis and is happy to help build relationships for his local staff. 'Even at chairman level,' says Harris, 'you must have an objective for the visit. We deliberately take the chairman somewhere where we need to improve our relationship.'

Chris McDonald of Rolex (Japan) Ltd agrees. 'The chairman of Rolex first came to Japan in 1955 and has been coming here every year since. This maintains the link we have with all our important clients. The Japanese want to meet the top dog. They want to see the evidence of our commitment to the market.' A British company executive in Tokyo told me that one of his American competitors was using the fact that the British chief executive had never visited Japan as proof that the company was not committed to the Japanese market, and that the Japanese should buy American instead.

If chief executives set the tone, then what can one think of another major British company, with a subsidiary and a joint venture long established in Japan, whose chief executive has not been there for almost 10 years? Does it really have the drive to succeed in Japan, or is the chief executive's inaction a sign of the complete confidence he has in those to whom he has delegated responsibility? In Japan, symbolic gestures are appreciated, and a company whose chief executive never goes east of Ramsgate is losing out on an opportunity to improve relationships and push a little deeper into the Japanese market.

Negotiating with the Government

There is no doubt that a single foreign company is at a huge disadvantage when negotiating with any part of the Japanese government. Such negotiations tend to take place however much you try to avoid them. A typical case might be for an approval from the Ministry of Health and Welfare to get foreign laboratory tests admitted as valid evidence. It could be as trivial as a discussion with the Ministry of Justice over a visa application or as important as talks with the Ministry of Posts and Telecommunications over the specification of a major communications network. In every case, a Japanese person or company would not negotiate. He would accept the view of the ministry as being unarguable. A Japanese knows that to get what you want from any part of the government, you have to fulfil every aspect of their requirements, without question. Any failure takes you back to the beginning.

This is not an attitude which comes naturally to foreigners, but if you are merely one company trying to make your way in Japan, the only advice is to follow the local rules. According to Shunya Miyazaki, Osaka representative for the Kent Enterprise Office and for many years a Mitsui Trading man with long hours of experience in dealing with Japanese bureaucracy, 'Japanese companies may give themselves a better lie by moving the ball six inches nearer the hole,' and the government acts as caddy. But it is very rare for Japanese industry to be in conflict with government, and it does no good for foreign companies to be in conflict with Japanese government. 'Some of this American head-on clash with Japan is just a matter of not knowing how to get on,' says Tim Bridgman of Swires. 'But the truth is that if something comes up, your Japanese competitor gets the first bite of the cherry.'

Clashes with the Japanese government should only be undertaken by foreign governments or by your competitors. Foreign governments might win, which may help your cause. Your competitors will certainly not win, which will help your cause even more.

The Negotiating Table

A meeting at a Japanese company has many similarities to the formal courtship dances of a highly plumed jungle bird. There is one obvious difference – the Japanese contingent will not be highly plumed in their grey or blue suits, their white shirts, black shoes and understated ties – but in the ritual of the performance, in the way that it leads slowly but inevitably to the point, and in the fact that nobody can tell at the outset when or where that point will be reached, a Japanese negotiation meeting is a stylised business dance.

After your prompt arrival at your Japanese counterpart's office, you will be shown into an empty meeting-room by a young office lady, who will then tell your hosts that you have arrived. The meeting-room will contain a low table, flanked by armchairs and a long sofa. While it is impolite to be seated when your hosts arrive, it is necessary to have decided which seats you will occupy. In Japan, it is polite for the host to sit with his back to the door, and for his guests to sit on the opposite side of the table. This custom dates back to medieval times when a lord would protect his visitors from sudden attack by an assassin by seating himself nearest the door and with his back to it. Any intruder would go for the nearest person first: the host. In fact, as most assassins in medieval castles were members of the guest's party, it was pretty certain they would go for their target, the host, first, wherever he was sitting, but the pretence had to be maintained and the custom remains. As a visitor, you will sit on the side of the table facing the door. Assassins paid by either side in a negotiation are rarer these days than they used to be 500 years ago.

It is important that your party all sit on the same side of the table. It is not right to split up either side in the negotiations. Once your hosts arrive, there will be an exchange of business cards (see Chapter Five) among those who have not met before, and then you sit down. At this point the meeting begins, but the first period is spent in small talk about everything except the subject on the agenda. A negotiation is no different from a routine meeting in this aspect, although after the first few meetings the need for probing questions about whether you have ever been up Tokyo Tower does seem to diminish.

It will also take a few meetings for you to sort out who exactly is who on the other side, but, looking at it from the Japanese side, they are also trying to discover the key players on your team. The Japanese like face-to-face meetings because it enables them to see you and your colleagues working together, and to assess the internal strength of the company as well as its external strength in its dealings with the rest of the market-place. They like to see a genuine team effort, so your negotiation should not seem like a one-man show, even if it is. Theirs may also be a one-man show, but you are unlikely ever to be sure which one man is the key man, even by checking the titles on the business cards or the way your hosts sit opposite you. The spokesman will almost never be the most senior, and will probably not be the most influential. He will merely be the one with the best English. It is also worth remembering that there may be conflicts of personality or of interest on the Japanese side just as there can be within a British negotiating team. 'The Japanese are great lovers of factions,' says Tim Bridgman of Swires, 'which can make rational decision-making not entirely rational.' One other European negotiating a joint venture tells of the level of disagreement almost bordering on hatred which he discovered existed between two of the Japanese negotiating team he was dealing with every day. His greatest difficulty from then on was not to fall into the easy habit of saying or doing things to accentuate this enmity. As a foreigner, it was not for him to take sides in what was clearly a longstanding feud.

Speak clearly and simply, always refer to your colleagues, and do not change a major negotiating position without taking advice outside the meeting. Negotiations make their own timetable, and there is no merit in being brash or trying to hurry things along. You will only hurry them into an unsatisfactory conclusion. However, if you have a strong position, hold it. Your Japanese opposite numbers certainly will. As negotiators they will be tough, unblinking in their determination to achieve their goal, but always aware of the need to create an agreement at the end of the negotiations that both sides can be happy with. If you take the same view before going into the meeting-room for the first time, you will improve your chances of success. You are negotiating a marriage, not a brief affair.

'If they have been really nice, if there has been lots of tea and coffee and the president has been wheeled in at the end of the meeting, you might as well forget it,' says George Newns. 'But if they've given you a tough time, asking lots of difficult questions, then they are interested.'

Negotiations take time, but if they reach a happy conclusion the president will be wheeled in, and your president should be wheeled in at an equal speed. The formal ceremony to announce the successful outcome of your negotiations will be held at a major Tokyo hotel, everybody in your box of name cards will be invited and large rosettes will be worn. Much of your first year's marketing budget will be used up. 'Will the book have a section on making public presentations and how you should not?' asked Geoffrey Breeze of the Hilton Group. 'Don't speak. Just cut the ribbon and get off.'

Japanese Businessmen in Britain

Most British businessmen come across the Japanese business community most often not in Tokyo but in Britain. Few companies can operate without direct contact with Japanese corporations in the UK. Doing business in Japan can be made easier by doing business with Japanese firms here.

'Get some practice in by dealing with Japanese companies in Britain,' suggests Andrew Lawson of the CBI. Build up the contacts which will turn into relationships which will turn one day into successful business partnerships.

Britain currently receives over one-third of all Japanese investment in Europe, and although there are signs that the total is beginning to slow down, Britain's share continues to outstrip that of our European partners. JETRO give several reasons, from the British government's attitude to inward investment to the quality of the British work-force. They also cite the fact that the City of

When a Japanese Company Visits Yours

Do

- Prepare meticulously
- Fly a Japanese flag, and if possible the Union Jack and your company flag
- Ensure all top-level managers are present to greet
- Show your visitors around your premises
- Be proud of your company, but modest about individuals
- Have full company information packs for each visitor
- Have a small flag set on the meeting-table
- Check whether an interpreter will be required
- Have an agenda prepared
- Have plenty of business cards
- Have an answer for every question, or a promise of an answer
- Answer the question asked, not the one you'd like to answer
- Avoid confrontation
- Show interest in Japan, your visitor's home and family
- Have something for them to take away as a souvenir of their visit

Don't

- Be disorganised
- Split up your visitors in the formal seating arrangements
- Allow interruptions for telephone calls or any other reason, apart possibly from a major fire in the office
- Slap people on the back, laugh over-heartily or talk in very colloquial language
- Write on your visitors business cards
- Worry if they talk amongst themselves in Japanese
- Try to pull the wool over your customer's eyes
- Contradict or be combative
- Get into political discussions unnecessarily
- Expect an order immediately
- Be surprised

(Source: UKOA Ltd 1991)

London is the financial centre of Europe, and, very importantly, that English is the native language. Britain is also seen as a pleasant place in which to live.

When you deal with Japanese business people in Britain, you do not have to worry about the etiquette of drinking Japanese tea or in which language to speak. On home ground you can play to British rules. However, the list of do's and don'ts on p. 139, prepared by UKOA, the cross-cultural business briefing organisation, can still help when you are acting as host to Japanese business visitors.

Doing Business In Japan – The Future

Where do we go from here? If Japan is changing as rapidly as the social scientists would have us believe, can we expect any of the experience of the past to work for us in the future? Will next year's ideas about Doing Business In Japan be necessarily entirely different from this year's? And what of the next century?

Japan is certainly changing, but then so is Britain and so is Europe in these post-Maastricht times, much more rapidly than Japan. Certain truths which have remained constant about Japan for several hundred years can be safely assumed to have relevance for a few more at least. Japan will always be a crowded country. The group consciousness will continue to take precedence over the individual consciousness, despite an increasing awareness of self-image. People will still tend to spend their entire careers with one organisation, because how to make that organisation work successfully is the most valuable skill a businessman can develop, and it only comes by using the relationships built on the experience of working there. Headhunting companies with names like Hop-Job may mushroom, but the one-company career will continue to be the norm. Japanese industry will continue to thrive because the Japanese place value on a successful and socially constructive business career. As more money flows through the Japanese economy and into the hands of consumers (and almost as quickly out again), we may see a decline in the percentages of money saved and a change in the type of products bought by consumers. But there will be no structural slow-down in the Japanese economy brought about by changes in the Japanese persona. International slumps and booms may affect the performance of the Japanese economy to a certain extent, but do not look for a completely new set of national values to revolutionise the way the economy fits into the global picture.

The British government's view is that there must be a more targeted approach in Anglo-Japanese trade. 'We are looking for a switch from hunting to farming,' says Paul Dimond at the Embassy in Tokyo. British companies must not just capture the business where they happen to find it, they must spend time developing and growing business opportunities in Japan. 'We must develop our products so that they fit into a global niche. If we rely only on "unique British technology", the law of diminishing returns will apply. The quality of demand in Japan is so high that success in Japan must lead to success world-wide. If your strategy is to find a global niche for your products, you will only achieve that if you come to Japan.'

Some commentators see a shrinking manufacturing base in Japan, on the theory that production will become too expensive to be done in that overcrowded country. They believe that the number of 'sunset' industries whose production moves offshore will grow rapidly. Graham Harris notes that, 'One theory is that manufacturing will move increasingly overseas, so that manufactured exports from Japan will be very low. Japanese technological skills will remain onshore, but manufacturing will be overseas.' This is not, however, what MITI intends. 'The lower end needs to be rationalised,' says Dimond, 'to release resources. For example, the number of people in distribution could profitably be reduced and the number of software engineers could be increased. The size of the manufacturing base will not shrink, but its nature will change, from a lower level to higher technology.'

What will not change is the need to succeed in business with the Japanese if you are to grow your business internationally. As Jeff Gale of the Exports To Japan Unit of the Department of Trade and Industry puts it, 'You will not find it easy to be successful in third country business on a long-term basis unless you have been successful in Japan.'

It Does Get Easier: A Few Random Opinions

'There is no secret about Japanese management practices. It's all common sense. Lifetime employment tends towards paternalism, but, even in Britain or America, if you treat your employees as human beings they are less likely to leave. It's all a matter of developing respect.'

'Our Japanese partners said to us, "You need to walk into the mist." You cannot have a completely clear picture of what lies ahead. We just had to get on and do it. We had to have faith in ourselves and our Japanese partners, and not worry about what could go wrong.'

'There are two kinds of foreign business executive in Japan. There are the ones who work closely with the Japanese, and there are those who come over like aliens and avoid as much direct contact as possible.'

'There are books and books and books about Japan. They are all different but they are all the same. There's no one story. But then it's the same in Britain. London and Liverpool are just as different as Tokyo and Osaka.'

'The books say there is no room in Japan for people like me, with experience but no official training in things Japanese. But there are no hard and fast rules. If they are sensitive to the Japanese way of doing business, there is room for anybody.'

'My Japanese secretary once said to me, "You are very decisive." This is not a compliment. You have to learn to let things happen.'

' "But a Japanese told me" is the favourite phrase of visitors who do not like what they are hearing from their man in Tokyo. If a Japanese told them, whoever it was, it must be right, even if their very expensive man in Tokyo tells them otherwise. How could a foreigner know better? But we are not a bunch of foreign eyes looking despairingly on from the outside. We are a Japanese corporation, which happens to be foreign-owned and with a *gaijin* president, but otherwise we are no different from any other Japanese entity.'

'If you can survive a year, it gets better. I hope so, anyway.'

'The question, "Is she a beautiful woman or not?" depends on the opinion of who is looking at her. Is Japan all a conspiracy? It depends on how you look at it.'

CHAPTER 9

SURVIVAL GUIDE

Some Japanese Phrases

Good morning	*Ohayo gozaimasu*
Good day	*Konnichi wa*
Good evening	*Komban wa*
Goodbye	*Sayonara*
I'm pleased to meet you	*Hajimemashite*
Thank you very much	*Domo arigato gozaimasu*
Don't mention it	*Do itashimashite*
Excuse me	*Sumimasen*
Sorry	*Shitsurei shimasu*
	Gomen nasai
Please	*Kudasai*
	Onegai shimasu
How are you?	*O genki desu ka?*
I am well	*Hai, genki desu*
How much is this?	*Kore wa ikura desu ka?*
Wait a moment, please	*Chotto matte kudasai*
I understand	*Wakarimashita*
I don't understand	*Wakarimasen*
Do your best!	*Gambare!*
Left/right/straight on	*Hidari/migi/massugu*
Telephone	*Denwa*
Train	*Densha*
Underground	*Chikatetsu*
Car	*Jidosha*
Expressway	*Kosoku Doro*
Limited company	*Kabushiki kaisha (KK)*
General trading company	*Sogo Shosha*
Joint venture company	*Goben kaisha*
Bank	*Ginko*

Chamber of Commerce	*Shoko kaigisho*
Embassy	*Taishikan*
Post Office	*Yubinkyoku*
Administrative guidance	*Gyosei shido*

How to get started

For basic information about the Japanese market, there are just four organisations you would be strongly advised to contact. In Britain the **Department of Trade and Industry Exports to Japan Unit** is the essential starting-point. The practical help they can give to businesses looking at Japan for the first or the 51st time is considerable, and the expertise they have available is formidable. No venture into the Japanese market should be made without the benefit of their resources. **JETRO (the Japan External Trade Organisation)** was established in 1958 to promote Japanese exports, but nowadays its mission is 'to support trade between Japan and other countries, with the aim of achieving balanced global trade'. They provide a great deal of information about the Japanese market and market opportunities through publications, seminars and individual briefings, and can be very helpful in setting up contacts.

In Japan, all British businessmen should check in at the **British Embassy Commercial Department**. The Embassy gives help and advice to all visiting businessmen who ask for it, and can provide more sophisticated support, such as market reports, etc., at a reasonable rate. The commercial staff is the most experienced and skilled of those in all our major diplomatic postings. The **British Chamber of Commerce in Japan** is an organisation to which virtually all British companies in Japan belong, as well as several UK-based companies with regular business contacts in Japan. They will provide help and practical guidance to newcomers, based on the experience of their members, which can be of great value. Anybody being posted to Japan should acquire a copy of their book *Japan Posting*, published in 1990, which is the fullest guide yet published to what living in Japan means for a foreigner.

It is also suggested that any visiting businessman drop in on his UK bank's Tokyo office, as this can often be a source of guidance and useful information.

Useful Addresses (Britain)

Government, official and non-profit-making bodies

Exports To Japan Unit
Department of Trade &
Industry
7F, Kingsgate House,
66–74 Victoria Street,
London SW1E 6SW
Tel: 071 215 5000
Fax: 071 215 2571
(Fairs and Promotion:
Tel: 071 276 2389)

Japan External Trade
Organisation (JETRO)
Leconfield House,
Curzon Street,
London W1Y 7FB
Tel: 071 493 7226
Fax: 071 491 7570

Japan Information and
Cultural Centre
Embassy of Japan
101 Piccadilly,
London W1V 9FN
Tel: 071 465 6500
Fax: 071 491 9348

Japan Chamber of Commerce
& Industry in UK
Rooms 493–495,
2F, Salisbury House,
29 Finsbury Circus,
London EC2M 5QQ
Tel: 071 628 0069
Fax: 071 628 0248

Japan National Tourist
Organisation
167 Regent Street,
London W1R 7FD
Tel: 071 734 9638
Fax: 071 734 4290

The Japan Foundation
17 Old Park Lane,
London W1Y 3LG
Tel: 071 499 4726
Fax: 071 495 1133

Anglo-Japanese Economic
Institute
Rooms 1–6,
2F, Morley House,
314–322 Regent Street,
London W1R 5AD
Tel: 071 637 7872
Fax: 071 636 3614

British Library
Japanese Information Service
25 Southampton Buildings,
Holborn,
London WC2A 1AW
Tel: 071 323 7465

Briefing, consulting and translating services

Centre For International
Briefing
Farnham Castle,
Farnham,
Surrey GU9 0AG
Tel: 0252 721194
Fax: 0252 711283

Euro-Japan Exchange
Foundation
Lane End,
near High Wycombe,
Bucks HP14 3HH
Tel: 0494 882091
Fax: 0494 882321

Japan Advisory Services
Fountain Precinct,
Balm Green,
Sheffield S1 1RZ
Tel: 0742 760351
Fax: 0742 725672

The Japanese Language
Association
Bath College of Higher
Education,
Sion Hill, Bath,
Avon BA1 5SF
Tel: 0225 483913
Fax: 0225 484594

SOAS
University of London,
Thornhaugh Street,
Russell Square,
London WC1H 0XG
Tel: 071 637 2388
Fax: 071 436 3844

Four By Four Consultancy
3 East Street, Alresford,
Hampshire SO24 9EE
Tel: 0962 735660
Fax: 0962 735670

Airlines

All Nippon Airways
2F, ANA House,
6–8 Old Bond Street,
London W1X 3TA
Tel: 071 915 3322
Fax: 071 915 3310

British Airways
Speedbird House,
Heathrow Airport,
Hounslow,
Middx TW6 2JA
Tel: 081 759 2525
Fax: 091 227 2865

Japan Airlines
Hanover Court,
5 Hanover Square,
London W1R 0DR
Tel: 071 408 1000

Virgin Atlantic Airways Ltd
Ashdown House,
High Street, Crawley,
West Sussex RH10 1DQ
Tel: 0293 747747
Fax: 0293 561721

In Japan

Government, official and non-profit-making bodies

Commercial Department
British Embassy,
1, Ichibancho,
Chiyoda-ku,
Tokyo 102
Tel: 03 3265 6340
Fax: 03 3265 5580

British Chamber of Commerce
in Japan
3rd Floor,
Kenkyusha Eigo Centre Bldg,
1–2 Kagurazaka,
Shinjuku-ku, Tokyo 162
Tel: 03 3267 1901
Fax: 03 3267 1903

British Consulate-General
Seiko Osaka Building
3–5–13 Bakuromachi,
Chuo-ku, Osaka 541
Tel: 06 281 1616
Fax: 06 281 1731

British Council
2 Kagurazaka 1-chome,
Shinjuku-ku, Tokyo 162
Tel: 03 3253 8031

British Council
77 Kitashirakawa Nishi-machi,
Sakyo-ku, Kyoto 606
Tel: 075 791 7151

Osaka Chamber of
Commerce & Industry
2–8 Hommachibashi,
Chuo-ku, Osaka 540
Tel: 06 944 6401

Japan External Trade
Organisation (JETRO)
2–5 Toranomon 2-chome,
Minato-ku, Tokyo 105
Tel: 03 3582 5511
Fax: 03 3587 0219

Immigration Bureau
Ministry of Justice
1–1 Kasumigaseki 1-chome,
Chiyoda-ku, Tokyo 100
Tel: 03 3580 4111

Ministry of International Trade
and Industry (MITI)
3–1 Kasumigaseki 1-chome
Chiyoda-ku, Tokyo 100
Tel: 03 3501 1511

Ministry of Finance
1–1 Kasumigaseki 3-chome,
Chiyoda-ku, Tokyo 100
Tel: 03 3581 4111

Law firms

Linklaters & Paines
3F, Mitsui Kyowa Building,
1–1 Kanda Suda-cho,
Chiyoda-ku,
Tokyo 101
03 3258 3691

Braun Moriya Hoashi & Kubota
Room 911, Iino Building,
1–1 Uchisaiwaicho 2–chome,
Chiyoda-ku,
Tokyo 100
03 3504 0251

Clifford Chance
6F South Hill Nagatacho
Building,
1–11–30 Nagata-cho,
Chiyoda-ku,
Tokyo 100
03 3581 4311

Accountants

Touche Ross
MS Shibaura Building,
4–13–23 Shibaura,
Minato-ku,
Tokyo 108
03 3457 1691

Arthur Andersen & Co.
Nihonseimei Akasaka Building,
8–1–19 Akasaka,
Minato-ku, Tokyo 107
03 3403 4211

Price Waterhouse
Aoyama Building,
1–2–3 Kita-Aoyama,
Minato-ku,
Tokyo 107
03 3404 9351

Useful addresses (Australia)

Japan External Trade
Organisation (JETRO)
Level 19, Gateway Building,
1 Macquarie Place,
Circular Quay,
Sydney 2000
02 241 1181

JETRO
4th Floor,
Standard Chartered House,
30 Collins Street,
Melbourne 3000
03 654 4949

JETRO
St Georges Court Building,
16 St Georges Terrace,
Perth WA 6000
09 325 2809

Japan Airlines
14th Floor Darling Park
201 Sussex Street,
Sydney 2000
02 268 9911

Japanese Consulate-General
52 Martin Place,
Sydney 2000
02 231 2455

Austrade
AIDC Tower Maritime
Centre,
201 Kent Street
Sydney 2000
02 390 2000

Qantas
203 Coward Street,
Mascot 2020
02 691 3636

Australian-Japan Society
of NSW
201 Kent Street,
Sydney 2000
02 299 2242

In Japan

Australian Trade Commission
Australian Embassy
2-1-14 Mita,
Minato-ku,
Tokyo 108
03 5232 4125

Australian Trade Commission
Australian Consulate-General
23rd Floor, Kokusai Building,
3–13 Azuchimachi 2-chome,
Chuo-ku, Osaka 541
06 271 7071

Useful addresses (New Zealand)

In New Zealand

JETRO Auckland
Room 301,
Dilworth Building,
Customs Street, E. Auckland
09 797 427

In Japan

New Zealand Trade
Development Board
New Zealand Embassy
20–40 Kimiyama-cho,
Shibuya-ku, Tokyo 150
03 3467 2271

Useful addresses (Canada)

Japan External Trade
Organisation (JETRO)
151 Bloor Street West,
Toronto, Ontario
M5S 1T7
416 962 5055

JETRO
660 World Trade Centre,
999 Canada Place,
Vancouver, British Columbia
V6C 3E1
604 684 4174

Japanese Consulate
Toronto Dominion Bank Tower,
Ste 2702, PO Box 10,
Toronto Dominion Centre,
Toronto, Ontario
M5K 1A1
416 363 7038

Japanese Consulate
Suite 900–1177 West Hastings
Street,
Vancouver, British Columbia
V6E 2K9
604 684 5868

Japan Air Lines
First Canadian Place
Street 1000
P.O. Box 115
Toronto, Ontario
M5X 1A4
416 364 7226

In Japan

Canadian Embassy
3–38 Akasaka 7-chome,
Minato-ku,
Tokyo 107
03 3408 2101

FURTHER READING

For further reading on Japan, we suggest the following books:

General reading:

Modern Japan, W. G. Beasley (Allen & Unwin, 1975)
The Chrysanthemum and the Sword, Ruth Benedict (1946)
The Japanese Today, Edwin O. Reischauer (Tuttle, 1988)
The Japanese Achievement, Hugh Cortazzi (Sidgwick & Jackson, 1990)
The Anatomy of Dependence, Takeo Doi (Kondansha, 1973)
Landscapes And Portraits, Donald Keene (Kondansha, 1971)
Japan Is a Circle, Kenichi Yoshida (Norbury, 1975)
Japan – The New Official Guide (Japan Travel Bureau Inc., 1990)
Japan – It's Not All Raw Fish, Don Maloney (Japan Times, 1975)

Business books:

Kaisha, The Japanese Corporation, James C. Ableggen and George Stalk Jr (Harper & Row, 1985)
Japan vs. The West, Endymion Wilkinson (Penguin, 1990)
Nippon: New Superpower, William Horsley and Roger Buckley (BBC Books, 1990)
Triad Power, Kenichi Ohmae (Macmillan, 1985)
The Mind of the Strategist, Kenichi Ohmae (Penguin, 1990)
The New Masters – Can The West Match Japan?, Philip Oppenheim (Business Books, 1991)
Japan Inc., Dr Max Eli (McGraw Hill, 1991)
The Sun Also Sets, Bill Emmott (Simon & Schuster, 1990)

Language books:

Kenkyusha's Japanese-English Dictionary
Nelson's Japanese-English Character Dictionary
Guide to Reading and Writing Japanese, Florence Sakade, ed. (Tuttle, 1959)

References

Apart from several of the above, the following books have been used as reference in the writing of this book:

Industrial Groupings in Japan (Dodwell Marketing Consultants, 1990)
Japan 1991 Marketing and Advertising Yearbook (Dentsu, 1991)
Japan Regional Investment Guide, The Challenge of the Japanese Market, Directory of Sources of Information and Business Services, Setting Up a Business in Japan (all JETRO, 1991)
Human Resources in Japan, Gaijin Scientist, Research and Development in Japan, Japan Posting (all British Chamber of Commerce in Japan, 1990, 1991)

Many publications by the Department of Trade and Industry Exports to Japan Unit, and by the Anglo-Japanese Economic Institute have also helped considerably. I have also referred to newspaper and magazine stories from, among others, the *Japan Times, Tokyo Weekender* and *Asahi Shimbun* in Tokyo, as well as the *Economist, The Times, Independent, Japan Digest, Focus Japan* and *Management Today* in Britain.

INDEX

Abegglen, James, 70
administrative guidance, 60–2
advertising, 112–17, 118–19, 124–5
agents, 83–5, 93
air travel, 77–8
Akihito, Emperor, 21
alphabets, syllabic, 30
amakudari, 58
Andoh, Andy, 65, 66
appointments, 74–5, 81

bankruptcies, 71
banks, 43, 64, 65, 71, 97, 99, 125
Barrett, Mike, 12, 39, 42, 45, 57, 98
Bedingham, Mark, 88–91, 115, 118–19
BMW, 134
body language, 31–2
brand names, 112, 116
Brankin, Maire, 110
Brankin, Dr Paul, 84, 85–6, 96–8, 99–101
Branson, Richard, 109
Breeze, Geoffrey, 122, 123–4, 138
bribes, 80
Bridgman, Tim, 11, 14, 39–40, 87, 136, 137
British Chamber of Commerce, 75, 97, 99
British Embassy, 75, 76, 84, 97
British Telecom, 94
bureaucracy, 57–9, 60–2
business cards, 25, 78–9, 137
business titles, 44–5
business trips, 73–8, 97

C. Itoh, 65, 120
Carlisle, Malcolm, 51, 95, 103–6, 131–2
cars, 9–10, 15, 35, 84–5, 112
chief executives, 134–5
Chisso, 118
civil servants, 57–9
Clifford, David, 111, 113, 114, 115
climate, 19–20
Coca-Cola, 16–17
communications, corporate, 118
commuting, 34
compact discs, 92, 111–12
Confederation of British Industry, 59
'Confucian Communism', 41
consensus, 47–52, 57, 60
consumers *see* customers
contracts, 132
Cornes, 84–5
corporate communications, 118
corporate structure, 42–5
credit cards, 76
cross-shareholding, 63–4
customers, 16, 43, 110–12, 125, 140
customs and excise, 87–8

debt:equity ratios, 71
decision-making, 13, 42–3, 47–52
Dentsu, 111, 112–15, 117
Dentsu Burson-Marsteller, 117–18
Department of Trade and Industry (DTI), 7, 9, 75, 76, 84, 141

de Stains, Ian, 75, 93, 95
Diet (parliament), 22
Dimond, Paul, 7–9, 14, 102, 140–1
direct marketing, 124–5
distribution, 90–1, 100
DKB, 63, 65
duty, wines and spirits, 89
Dyson, Tony, 86–7

earthquakes, 20–1
economy, 15–16
education, 36–8, 54, 57
etiquette, 78–83, 139
European Community (EC), 89, 101
exhibitions, 76
exports, 5–10, 73–92
eye contact, 32

Fair Trade Commission (FTC), 101
finance, business trips, 76–7
food, 35–6
Fuji bank, 63
Fuyo, 63

Gale, Jeff, 141
GATT, 89
general trading companies, 65–6, 83–6
geography, 19–21
gifts, 80, 111
GNP, 15
Gordon, James, 107
government, 22–3, 57–60, 135–6
grants, DTI, 76
group dependency, 24–5
Grundy, Tony, 61–2, 107–8
Guinness, Helen, 39, 45, 62

Hakuhodo, 112–13, 114, 115

Hama, Noriko, 52–3, 55, 56
Handl, Richard, 122
Harris, Graham, 17, 18, 28, 29–30, 66, 134–5, 141
Harris, Kyoko, 80
head office, 134–5
Hideyoshi, Toyotomi, 45–6
Hilton Hotels, 122–4
history, 21–2
Hokkaido, 19, 40
holidays, national, 74
Honda, 10
Honshu, 19, 120–1
hotels, 73–4, 76–7, 122–4
housing, 33–4

Ieyasu, Tokugawa, 45–6
importers, 83–5
industry, structure, 57–72
information, 121
Inman, Mike, 27, 28, 36, 125, 126
insurance, 86–7, 125
international trade, 5–10
interpreters, 29
investment, foreign, 16
investor relations, 118
itineraries, 74–5

Japan Association of Corporate Executives, 59
Japan Chamber of Commerce and Industry, 59
Japan External Trade Organisation (JETRO), 9, 75, 84, 97, 132, 138–9
Japan Federation of Employers' Associations, 59
Japan Inc., 57–60
Japan Medico, 102–6, 130
Jardines Wines & Spirits, 88–91, 111, 115, 118–19
jet lag, 77–8
joint ventures, 93, 101–6, 108–9, 131

Kaifu, Toshiki, 23
Kanematsu Gosho, 65
Kansai, 120–1
Keidanren, 59

Keiretsu, 62–70
Keizai Doyukai, 59
Kennedy, George, 104
KK (limited company), 94–5
Koito, 102, 114
Kuraray, 102–5, 131
Kurita, Nobufumi, 54, 55, 56, 132

labels, 112
labour relations, 71–2
language, 11–12, 27–32, 116, 119, 131–2, 139
Large, Dick, 17, 129
Lawson, Andrew, 26, 80, 130, 138
lawyers, 61–2, 94–5, 106–8, 131–2
left-handedness, 81
leisure activities, 25–6
Liberal Democratic Party (LDP), 22–3
lifetime employment, 41–2
limited companies, 94–5
Linklaters & Paines, 61–2, 106–7
Lloyd-Hughes, Tim, 3

McCann Erickson, 114
McDonald, Chris, 115, 135
McDonald's, 17
madogiwazoku ('window people'), 127–8
mail order, 124–5
management styles, 39–41, 45–7
market research, 55, 84
market share, 70–1
marketing, 110–17, 123–5
Marubeni, 65, 120
Marui, 109, 125
Matsushita, 67, 68, 112, 120
medical devices, 102–6
meetings, 15, 74–5, 81, 126–40
meishi (business cards), 25, 78–9
Mikami, Hiroshi, 92, 102–4, 130
Ministry of Finance, 62

Ministry of International Trade and Industry (MITI), 62, 66, 141
missions, trade, 76
Mitsubishi Group, 42, 52–3, 55, 63, 64, 65, 66, 68, 69, 112
Mitsui & Co., 14, 63, 65, 66, 103
Miyazaki, Shunya, 136
Miyazawa, Prime Minister, 38
money, business trips, 76–7
Moss, Chris, 17, 28, 35, 77, 78
Murakamo, Yoichiro, 70
Muramatsu, Shinobu, 64

Nakamura, Akira, 125
Nakamura, Hiroshi, 122, 123, 124
Narita airport, 77, 78
negotiations, 47–51, 126–40
nemawashi, 14–15, 47–51
Newns, Dr George, 11–12, 14, 29, 94, 126, 138
Nichimen, 65
Nikkeiren, 59, 71
Nippon Steel, 68
Nissan, 68, 71–2, 116
Nissho Iwai, 65
'no', 49, 51
Nobunaga, Oda, 45–6

Okinawa, 19, 40
open market, 92
Osaka, 19, 20, 34, 40, 41, 73, 119–21
Oxford Instruments, 85–6, 95–8, 99–101

packaging, 111–12
parallel imports, 85, 91
Parker, Sir Peter, 4
parliament, 22
Pearce, Bob, 28, 65–6, 83, 84–5, 129
Pharmaceutical Affairs Law, 60–1
Pickens, T. Boone, 102, 114
Plaistow, David, 85

politics, 22–3
pollution, 34
population, 21
Portex, 102–5, 130
premises, 99
presents, 80, 111
prices, 129
Procter & Gamble, 7
profit motive, 70–1
public relations, 117–19
public transport, 34, 35
punctuality, 81

railways, 34, 35
rank, 45
recruiting staff, 97–9, 101
relationships, 25–7, 39
representative offices, 93–94
retirement, 38
ringi system, 50–1
Rokudai Kigyo Shudan (Six Major Industrial Groups), 63, 66
Rolex, 115, 135
Rolls Royce, 84–5, 112
Rover Group, 10
Ryukyu Islands, 19

sales promotion, 110–17
Sanwa, 63
Sanyo, 120
sarariman (businessman), 32–6
Sawa, Takamitsu, 121
service, 110–11
shareholders, 43, 63–4, 70–1, 118
Shikoku, 19, 40, 120–1
shipping goods, 96–8
shops, 36, 111–12

'silver agers', 38
Smiths Industries (SIMS), 102–6, 131
Social Democratic Party (SDP), 23
society, 24–7
Sony, 51, 120
specifications, 52
sponsors, 95
sports, 25–6
staff: corporate communications, 118; lifetime employment, 41–2; recruiting, 97–9, 101
Stalk, George Jr, 70
strikes, 71–2
subsidiaries, 93–101
Sumitomo Corp., 41, 54, 63, 65, 68, 120
syllabaries, 30

take-over bids, 63–4, 102
taxation, 89, 94
taxis, 35, 78
tea-drinking, 82–3
television, 115, 117
Teno, Mie, 55
Thompson, J. Walter, 114
Thorne, Ben, 14, 17–18, 40, 57, 58, 59, 60, 80, 126, 127, 128–9, 130
Thorneycroft, Lord, 32
titles, business, 44–5
Tokyo, 19, 20, 34–5, 40, 73, 77, 78, 99, 119–20, 121–2
Tokyo Stock Exchange, 58
Toshiba, 68
Toyo Keizai Shimpo-sha, 58

Toyo Menka, 65
Toyota, 55, 68, 72, 83–4
trade, international, 5–10
trade missions, 76
trade unions, 71–2
trading companies, 65–6, 83–6
traveller's cheques, 76
travelling to Japan, 77–8

unions, 71–2
universities, 37–8, 53

Virgin Group, 92, 108–9, 111–12, 125
visas, 73

Wada, Ryosuke, 119
weather, 19–20
whisky, 88–90
Whitehorn, Will, 28, 108–109
wholesalers, 90–1
Williams, Gordon, 51, 83–4, 120, 125
Williams, Peter, 96
'window people', 127–8
wines and spirits, 88–91
women, 12, 52–6
work ethic, 39–56
writing, 29–31

yakuza, 80
Yasuda, 63
Yates, Rosemary, 56, 129, 130–1, 133
'yes', 49–50
Yoshida, Hiromi, 40, 114–15, 116–17, 119
Young & Rubicam, 114

zaibatsu, 62–3